Literature, Disaster, and the Enigma of Power:
A Reading of *Moby-Dick*

Literature, Disaster, and the Enigma of Power

A Reading of 'Moby-Dick'

Eyal Peretz

STANFORD UNIVERSITY PRESS
STANFORD, CALIFORNIA

Stanford University Press
Stanford, California
© 2003 by the Board of Trustees of the
Leland Stanford Junior University
Printed in the United States of America

Library of Congress Cataloging-in-Publication Data

Peretz, Eyal.
 Literature, disaster, and the enigma of power : a reading of
'Moby-Dick' / Eyal Peretz.
   p. cm.
 Includes bibliographical references and index.
 ISBN 0-8047-4614-1 (cloth : alk. paper)
 ISBN 0-8047-8709-3 (pbk. : alk. paper)
 1. Melville, Herman, 1819–1891. Moby Dick. 2. Melville,
Herman, 1819–1891—Political and social views. 3. Sea stories,
American—History and criticism. 4. Power (Social sciences) in
literature. 5. Whaling in literature. 6. Whales in literature.
I. Title.
PS2384.M62 P47   2003
813'.3—dc21   2002012995

This book is printed on acid-free, archival-quality paper.

Original printing 2003

Designed and typeset at Stanford University Press in 11/15 Garamond

To the memory of my grandmother, FRIEDA
To my parents, OFRA *and* DANNY
And to my brother, ASSAF

Acknowledgments

This book, which is a development of my dissertation thesis, is first and foremost the fruit of an encounter with two inspiring teachers. Shoshana Felman—being guided by the enigmatic lucidity and demanding emotional rigor of her teaching, her courage of thinking, and her humanity, has been for me a transforming event, and Irad Kimhi—whose infinite capacity for understanding, extraordinary joy in thinking, and profound friendship, have taught me what a philosophical life could mean.

I am extremely grateful to Stanley Cavell, whose generosity of spirit and uniquely democratic philosophical sensibility has been a constant force in shaping my work. I would also like to thank Wai-Chee Dimock for her encouragement and help during the last stages of writing this book.

I finally wish to thank a few of my friends who over the years read numerous versions of this book in various stages, helping to improve it substantially: I would especially like to acknowledge Ulrich Baer for his remarkable dedication to this book and his constant willingness to help improve it. I would also like to thank Lance Duerfahrd, Ido Geiger, Jim Gibbons, Luc Kinsch, and Emily Sun.

Contents

Introduction   1
    From Judgment to Power, 3
    America—A Witnessing of Europe, 19

1 The Enigma of Power   27

2 Call Me Ishmael   35
    Leviathanalysis, 46

3 Ahab's Whale—A Bleeding Wound   48
    Language as Hunt; Language as Wail, 54

4 Ishmael's Whale—Whiteness and the Witness, or the Collapse of the Author   67
    The Power of Whiteness, 68
    Two Understandings of the Fabulous, 86
    Moby-Dick and Literary History, 90
    Ishmael: Whale-Author(ity), 98
    Coda, 118

Notes   121
Bibliography   165
Index   173

Literature, Disaster, and the Enigma of Power:
A Reading of *Moby-Dick*

Introduction—Performing the Whale: Moby-Dick's Wounding of Literature

> Of course it is true that only in Melville's book does Ahab meet Moby Dick; yet it is also true that only this encounter allows Melville to write the book, it is such an imposing encounter, so enormous, so special that it goes beyond all the levels on which it takes place, all the moments in time where we attempt to situate it, and seems to be happening long before the book begins, but it is of such a nature that it also could not happen more than once, in the future of the work and in that sea which is what the work will be, having become an ocean on its own scale.
> —Maurice Blanchot, *The Song of the Sirens*

> Profound aversion to reposing once and for all in any one total view of the world. Fascination of the opposing point of view: refusal to be deprived of the stimulus of the enigmatic.
> —Nietzsche, *The Will to Power*

This book is an attempt to respond to a nineteenth-century American novel, Herman Melville's *Moby-Dick*, and to the demand that it makes on us to rethink what literature might mean for our times.

Our period is one of an intense problematization and putting into question the traditional status and function of literature. Writers of highly divergent styles and quite different theoretical approaches share a feeling that something happened and that literature, or at least the understanding and the reading of literature, can not, and must not, go on as it did before. We might say, more dramatically, that it is now necessary to explode the traditional conception of literature.

We might thus put side by side as participating in this contemporary questioning of literature such writers as Artaud—who castigates the European conception of art as corrupt and deadening and challenges the authority of its historical monuments and the values they represent under the slogan "no more masterpieces"—and Celan—whose enigmatic poetry struggles with, and testifies to, the condition famously articulated by Adorno's statement that after Auschwitz it is no longer possible to write poems. Nietzsche—who calls for a renewed and expanded understanding of art as the expression of the Will to Power and as an enhancement of life, to be turned against the moralistic/ philosophic resentment of life—is related to Heidegger's and Derrida's attempts at a destruction and a deconstruction of the metaphysical/aesthetic conception of literature and art which has dominated the West since at least Plato. Sartre—who attempts to define a politically engaged role for the work of literature— can join more recent theoretical enterprises such as New Historicism and Post-Colonial studies—that are trying to show literature's implication with, dependence upon and influence on various extraliterary discourses that form the context from which literature emerges and from which it has vainly tried to separate itself; these critical schools question the established hierarchy and center of the literary "canon," and the very idea of the "canon," in order to better listen to hitherto repressed and silent, "minor," voices lost in the margins.

I propose that it is within the context of this contemporary contestation of the traditional status of literature and art—mainly a development of twentieth-century Europe and raised in the wake of its disastrous history—that *Moby-Dick* demands to be read, and it is the nature of *Moby-Dick*'s challenge to, or even wounding of, our traditional conception of literature that I wish to examine in this book.

From Judgment to Power

Before beginning to discuss *Moby-Dick*, I would like to first invoke a twentieth-century European figure, whose complex experience and articulation of the contemporary crisis of literature, whose existential pathos and fury are particularly close to Melville's, and whose positioning of the problem of literature can guide us in attempting to approach Melville. This figure is Antonin Artaud.

"At a time when life itself is in decline," writes Artaud, "there has never been so much talk about civilization and culture. And there is a strange correlation between this universal collapse of life at the root of our present-day demoralization, and our concern for a culture that has never tallied with life but is made to tyrannize life. . . . It was our western idea of art and the profits we sought to derive from it that made us lose true culture. Art and culture cannot agree, contrary to world-wide usage! True culture acts through power and exaltation, while *the European ideal of art aims to cast us into a frame of mind distinct from the power present in its exaltation*. It is a useless, lazy idea and soon leads to death." It is to this anticipated return to life and this craved for experience of art, or true culture, as power and exaltation that Artaud calls "theatre": "For theatre, just as for culture, the problem remains to designate and direct shadows. And theatre, not confined to any fixed language or form, destroys false shadows because of this and prepares the way for another shadowed birth, uniting the true spectacle of life around it. To shatter language in order to contact life means creating or recreating theatre."[1]

Artaud's wail for a theatre to come, for a poetry of the future, uttered by a witness to cultural and personal disaster who is "like those tortured at the stake, signaling through the flames," marks the *problem* which the status of the literary and artistic work poses for us in a double manner: On the one hand literature and art as they exist in their traditional European conception are deemed obsolete, irrelevant to the surrounding horrors and the collapse of life in the midst of which we find ourselves;[2] and even more severely, they are *accused* of performing a terrible injustice in relation to our reality and even of cooperating in bringing about this catastrophic state which is our present condition.[3] On the other hand, it is precisely the work of literature and art, often designated as "theatre" in Artaud's case, that is invoked all the more urgently in the face of the present disaster,[4] and perhaps in a more complex manner it is *only* through and in the work of art that the disaster can be fully heard, witnessed, and uttered in a way which will do justice to it;[5] and going even further it is as if the work of art and literature is the place which holds for us, through the *literary* (or *theatrical*) witnessing of the disaster or catastrophe, the promise of a renewal of life and a revolution of our existence.

Although I see Artaud's position as particularly profound and complex, I also consider it representative of a certain contemporary attitude in relation to literature. I would therefore assume in the following discussions a double attitude which, on the one hand, follows and further develops Artaud's insights, and, on the other hand, traces a few points of their intersection with—and divergence from—other possible contemporary encounters with the problem we call literature.

I would thus like to isolate five issues and questions (out of many others) raised by this brief encounter with the way in which literature and art[6] open up as a problem for Artaud, five issues and questions that will guide this introduction and adumbrate what is at stake in my later reading of *Moby-Dick*: 1) Without giving any content yet to the term "literature," and before making a decision about what literature might or might not mean, we can already say that literature in our times finds itself in a position which can be characterized as that of an accused. That is, an implicit scene of judgment seems to be staged around the question of literature and art.[7]

Yet the question necessarily arises: by whom and in the name of whom or what is literature accused, and what authority judges it, if judgment always presupposes an authority capable of pronouncing a verdict? Paradoxically, it is only by reaching a decision regarding the authority in the name of which literature is judged that a decision about what literature might be can be given, since the very terms of the accusation presuppose—and thus in fact, in undefined cases such as literature is for us, performatively create—an identity that can bear the accusation. Assuming that there are no ideal and objective Platonic authorities—such as the Good, the Just, the True, etc.—in the name of which literature could be judged, there seem to be two possible approaches to this question implicit in Artaud regarding the status of literature as an accused. The first would judge literature on the basis of a certain extraliterary discourse about which terms are to count as authoritative and which are not, be it a discourse of social justice, a political discourse, a legal one, a historical discourse, or an ethical one, etc.

In this case, literature could be, and has been, found either not political enough, not ethical enough, etc. or inversely—which is the other side of the same coin—political through and through, historical through and through despite its pretense to distinction which is hence found to be illusory and dangerous.

This kind of judgment presupposes that a) the identity and function of these non-literary discourses as well as of literature and art are clear and stable and that either a clear-cut demarcation between the separate kinds of discourses or a straightforward unification of these discourses can be established; b) there is some common authority which all these discourses recognize and in whose processes of decision they can participate.

The second option implicit in Artaud seems to be that in some strange way *literature itself accuses and judges literature*, that there is something "within" literature "itself," and which can be heard *only* "within" literature itself, which has the sole authority to judge literature or a certain conception of literature.[8] But what strange kind of authority would come into being only within literature itself, and perhaps *as* literature itself, and which consequently can have no external viewpoint to literature itself from where it could be legitimated, and perhaps not even an external point of view from which its existence can be recognized? Is this authority still at all an authority in our usual understanding of the term, and is the judgment brought forth in its name still at all a judgment, at least as the term is usually understood in relation to legal terminology and conceptualization?[9]

This scene of judgment in which literature stands accused thus implicates the question of literature with the question of authority.

2) If literature, or something heard from within literature, is the sole "judge" of literature, then this means that literature is beyond or in excess of itself. That is, literature is in excess of any stable place or identity which can be called literature, and thus also in excess of any kind of external, non-literary, authority which would be able to demarcate what is literature and what is not. "Literature," and it is a question whether this name is to be kept, has lost a stable place to which it could be assigned—for example by treating works of literature as beautiful objects, as pleasing objects, as fictional discourses, etc.—and is drifting in search of a new destiny. How can we think this new destiny?

It is this feeling of excess, I suggest, that is also the feeling of the homelessness and of the new orphaned condition of literature, which is at the origin of contemporary attempts to think literature together with various non-literary discourses: literature-with-philosophy, with-law, with-history, with-medicine, with-the-political, etc.

This thinking-with at its profoundest is not merely a study of the mutual implication of two stable identities, but rather involves a complex operation of a simultaneous approaching and distancing whereby both—or all, in case there are more than two—discourses lose their stable place and identity, are de-centered, search in each other the source and perhaps the solution to their restlessness, are mutually transformed, yet also keep their distance and remain in suspension, their identities still in question. For this excess discovered through literature displaces and makes tremble not only literature itself, but also every other non-literary discourse along with it.

For at the moment when we don't know where literature belongs we obviously cannot know where it doesn't belong or interfere, what is not literature, and every discourse is in danger of being infiltrated. The setting loose of literature might thus involve a catastrophe for everybody involved. And this potential catastrophe (which, in a way, has already happened) points to a future reconfiguration of all discourses where neither literature, nor any other discourse, can remain recognizable in the terms used to understand them at present.[10]

3) We have seen that for Artaud this questioning of the status of literature depends on the question of disaster, or catastrophe. A rethinking of the status of literature, I suggest, involves a rethinking of the notion of disaster; or otherwise put, what we usually call literature has a particular and privileged affinity with the question of disaster. This relation between literature and disaster implies a double movement. It implies that through the exploration of literary language we can learn most profoundly about the crucial dimensions and consequences of disasters. But it also implies that the question of disaster explored in relation to literature brings about a transformation in our understanding of literature and puts into question all the traditional categories through which the literary has been thought.

This rapprochement between the questions of literature and disaster which has been pointed to, for example, by such theoreticians as Maurice Blanchot, seems to me to participate in a large intellectual movement that over the last fifty years has been increasingly transforming the traditional theoretical fields, from philosophy to law, to history, to literary theory. Indeed, I suggest, it might be possible to speak of a *catastrophic turn*—in the way that one used to talk of the linguistic turn—in the realm of thinking and in the concepts and the problems that the various theoretical discourses had to face. That is, the consequences of the violence and catastrophes of the twentieth century reached beyond the material and historical conditions of life and have had profound *conceptual* implications.

Artaud associates this notion of disaster invoked by the thought of literature or "theatre" with, among others, the figure of the cry[11] and the concept of life.[12] It will be a task of my discussion of *Moby-Dick* to develop these notions and the relations between them.

Yet I have also suggested that for Artaud, in a way, this disaster, and we might now also say life, or cry, can *only* be heard "within" literature, or *as* literature (or "theatre"). If this is the case, it would mean that the disaster could not be made available to anyone and to everyone unless they somehow *participate* in the literary or theatrical work. That is, this "experience" of the disaster or of the cry cannot be mediated as knowledge—which is in principle available to everyone even without having to acquire it, since it is by nature a communicable objective universality which depends on, and should in principle be guaranteed by, an original source of authority[13]—but rather has to have the character of a *singular event* which must be endured and whose existence cannot be guaranteed except through participation in its occurrence.[14]

What name should we give to the one who thus participates in an event that signals a break in the possibility of knowledge? Who is the one who hears the cry and participates in the disaster? Some recent thinkers such as Levinas, Derrida, Lyotard, Agamben, or Felman[15] have been increasingly paying attention to the development of the notion or the category of the *witness*. Usually associated with the legal realm signifying the one brought as a third party in front of the judging authority to report on knowledge unavailable to others, the term is undergoing a change of status, a transformation.

This new notion of the witness, which always implies a witnessed event and demands a thinking and a "logic" of the event, has many implications, but for our purposes I propose to synthesize what I grasp as taking place among these thinkers, though not necessarily articulated by them, by isolating four major implications:

a) The witness's language suffers, and thus signifies, a collapse in the vocabulary of knowledge, a collapse that has to do with a certain *excess* of the event witnessed beyond the witness's capacity to know the event. The event cannot be grasped and assimilated as knowledge because it overwhelms the witness. b) The witnessing act implies *singularity*. In some strange way what the witness testifies to is available in principle *only* to her or him, it is a secret that singularizes the witness. c) The witness feels obliged and even commanded to testify, yet it is not at all clear for the sake of which *authority* she or he is witnessing and in the name of what authority is her or his testimony to be accepted, for this singular testimony cannot be validated in the manner of usual legal testimonies, in which a judge assumes that the witness's knowledge is in principle available to all. The witness thus seems to imply a new kind of authority, or something different from authority altogether, which emanates from itself and cannot be guaranteed by any other authority. d) The witness is not external to the events upon which she or he reports, is not a *spectator*, but is implicated in them, participates in them, and is transformed by them. Or in other words, the witness is personally *addressed* by the events and what is at stake in her or his relation to the event is *who* she or he is.

I would thus suggest that the new, or rethought, position of the reader, of the one whose relation to the work of literature can only be that of participation in the event of disaster or the cry heard "within" it, is that of the witness. And, furthermore I suggest that this kind of witnessing to a disaster can only occur as "literature."

4) Yet this new notion of the reader/witness has another significant dimension that involves the implication and participation of the witness in the event and the enigmatic relation between passivity and activity this entails. On the one hand, we might say, becoming a witness implies absolute passivity in relation to the event witnessed. The witness in the new sense that I attempt to develop and to theorize has become so only due to an excess of the event that she or he cannot master or know. The witness, I propose, is the one constituted or called for by this unmasterable excess. She or he is thus always a *witness in spite of herself or himself,* against her or his will, like a prophet chosen to deliver a message who experiences this election as a curse or a malediction since it does not originate in her or his will and disorients the very basis of her/his existence.

Yet, on the other hand, becoming a witness implies an imperative to action. A witness is not a witness unless s/he has experienced the passive relation to the excess of the event as, precisely and paradoxically, a call to testify, that is to communicate, to transmit the excess which overwhelmed her/him, and in a way to transform through this transmission her/his addressees, to make them participants in the excess that revolutionized her/him. It is not that there is first an overwhelming event, which the witness can then decide to report or not to report; the excess of the event *can only be witnessed* through the transformation of the recipient of the event into the one who testifies. *There is no event outside of its transmission.*[16]

What name should we give to this witness whose passive exposure to the excess of the event which s/he can neither master nor know is at the same time and inextricably an "activity" of transmission and a command to transform? Who is this witness that announces what we glimpsed at in Artaud as the poetry of the future or the theatre to come? It is, I suggest, the *actor*, or the *performer*. If the excess of the event, which I have also designated following Artaud as disaster or cry, can only be heard through the coming into being of a witness who communicates that event, and if the witness can neither know nor master this disaster or cry but has to transmit it, then we might say that the only way both to receive and transmit the cry would be to *become* the cry or the disaster in the way that an actor assumes a role from which s/he becomes indistinguishable. *The witness is an actor of the disaster or the cry.*

Of course the understanding of the actor's relation to her/his role has to be changed. The actor is not someone who chooses this or that role at will as one changes clothes and who has a separate existence from her/his role. Neither is s/he someone who empathizes or "identifies" with a stable identity of a character s/he has to assume, à la Stanislavsky. Rather, the actor, I propose, is a witness to the role that transformed her or him into an actor through its assumption and transmission; and the *act of becoming an actor signifies that the relation of the witness to the disastrous excess which has to be transmitted but cannot be known is that of performance.*[17]

The witness performs and in this way transmits the excess of the disastrous event; and the recipients of this performance are called in their turn not to remain spectators but to become themselves performers, to further act the disaster. *Performance in this new understanding happens only when something cannot be communicated as knowledge*. I thus argue that the new position of the work of art and of its recipient, of the one implicated in a disastrous event which cannot be known but in which one has to participate, is that of the witness/performer or actor, and I also suggest that if literature involves the performance of a disaster then the disaster *intrinsically and essentially possesses a performative dimension and that the main category through which to think what has been called the performative dimension of literary language is the category of disaster and the question of its transmission*.[18]

5) As we have seen, this call for the transformation of the work of art and the discovery of the excess that is the consequence of its new orphaned condition involves for Artaud *a need to think art as power and exaltation, or as related to the vocabulary of power and force*. What is the significance of this transition, why should power become a privileged vocabulary through which to think the literary event?

"Power" is usually invoked in relation to the question of political power and in attempts to understand the nature and functioning of the political sphere. Yet it has been an attempt of several Nietzsche inspired contemporary writers (Foucault, Deleuze, Derrida, de Man), along with writers from other traditions (such as the speech-act philosopher J. L. Austin), to develop a thought of power and of force, or at least to resort to the vocabulary of power and force, as something which isn't necessarily and immediately related to the question of the political, but as *something which signals an irreversible break with the vocabulary of knowledge* and announces a new logic of thinking.[19] Thus Paul de Man, thinking about the question of history, says: "There is history from the moment that words such as 'power' and 'battle' and so on emerge on the scene. At that moment things *happen*, there is *occurrence*, there is *event*. History is therefore not a temporal notion . . . **but is the emergence of a language of power out of a language of cognition.**"[20] And Gilles Deleuze, in his book on Foucault, writes: "Power relations are not known. . . . instead it *[power] signifies another domain, a new type of relations, a dimension of thought that is irreducible to knowledge.*"[21]

If literature as a singular event opens up for us as a problem through a challenge to the vocabulary of knowledge, a challenge which at the same time raises the question of authority, then it would seem that the question of literature should be regarded as a privileged place *from which to think power as a question*, a central locus from which to articulate this new dimension of thought which the language of power seems to promise. Yet most recent discussions of literature's relation to power, usually inspired by Foucault's analysis of power though not necessarily constituting the best interpretation of their relevance to the question of literature, have mainly tried, through a staging of an implicit scene of judgment of literature in the manner I have pointed to above, to expose literature as cooperating with and participating in the mechanisms of power, understood as political power, from which literature vainly tries to separate itself.

That is, power in these discussions is not so much positioned as a problem and a promise for a new dimension of thought as it is offered as an answer and an instrument of judgment. Moreover, this exclusive identification of power with the question of the political, in which both terms are treated as more or less understood, neglects the possibility of thinking the political from the perspective of a new understanding of power which literature might open. For it is not at all certain that we know what the political is, and *it might thus be that a new thinking of literature announces a new thinking of the political.*

I would suggest that Hannah Arendt poses the question of the political for our times in a manner that is very close to Artaud's posing of the question of literature. For Arendt, the contemporary question of the political opens under the sign of disaster. The political for her is that which, on the one hand, has become completely suspect in our time and is accused of responsibility for this condition of disaster which is our life; yet, on the other hand, it is that whose rediscovery in its full significance holds for us, in the manner of a "miracle"—a miracle she calls freedom and which can occur *only* as political—a promise for a renewal of life and a revolution in our existence:

> The question we are posing results from very real political experiences we have endured. It results from the disaster that politics has already brought about in our century and from the even greater disaster that threatens to transpire from politics.[22] If, then, taking account of the impasse our world has reached, it is only befitting that we wait for miracles, in no way does this wait send us out of the original political sphere. If the meaning of politics is freedom, then this signifies that we have the right to *wait for a miracle in this sphere, and in this sphere only.*[23]

What is the relation between this miracle that can happen only as the political and the miracle or the event that can happen only as literature? This is perhaps the question for a thinking to come of the literary-with-the-political.

Let us briefly look at a particularly influential theoretical position that seems to me representative of the insufficiently problematized and somewhat reductive analyses of the relations among literature, the question of power, and the question of the political characterizing recent literary criticism.

Stephen Greenblatt, in "Power, Sexuality, and Inwardness in Wyatt's Poetry," an essay about the Renaissance writer Sir Thomas Wyatt which examines the implication of literature with political power and thinks against the modern understanding of literature as an autonomous aesthetic realm in which objects are created by a sovereign subject, writes: "Diplomacy, then, along with courtiership, seems to have influenced Wyatt's conception of the essential function of discourse, which he grasped as a shifting, often devious series of strategic maneuvers designed to enhance the power of the speaker, or rather of the party whom the speaker represents, at the expense of the power of some other party. The distinction between the speaker and the power he represents is worth emphasizing, for it is produced at the level of court poetry; that is, *the poem itself is a kind of agent, sent forth to perform the bidding of its master* . . . it is governed by its overarching purpose *which is to enhance its creator's personal position, to manifest and augment his power* . . . *Wyatt's poetry serves a* . . . *function* in relation to his position at court; and even at a distance from the court, in the psalms and satires, it is above all *power that shapes his poetic discourse*[24] . . . criticism has treated Wyatt's remarkable translations as a *purely literary affair*, whereas in fact *their very existence almost certainly depends on his ambassadorial experience.*"[25]

Exposing thus what might have pretended to be, or perceived by later generations to be, a purely literary affair—what Greenblatt understands as an autonomous aesthetic-formal affair—to the actual "fact" of political power and the context of interested motivations which are the exclusive concerns of this political power, Greenblatt testifies to the contemporary restlessness regarding the traditional status of the literary and to the feeling that a rethinking of the relations of, and the dissolution of traditional boundaries between, traditional discourses is called for. And he also testifies to the feeling that this change of status of the literary implies a demand to think it in relation to the question of power.

Nevertheless, it seems to me, Greenblatt does not go far enough, for behind the attempt of a dissolution and complication of the discourses lies a still much too traditional and stable identity of two discourses, which are the aesthetic and the political. Thus, if the aesthetic has to be problematized, it can only be so for Greenblatt in the name of another stable realm, the political, which itself does not seem at all disturbed by what has happened, but remains content in its sovereign power. And the aesthetic itself is still conceived as a possibly stable realm, as if the infiltration by the political has not completely destroyed the logic of what the aesthetic, and the political, might be.

Thus Greenblatt can half-heartedly speak about "the tendency to read back into the Renaissance the modern notion—not wholly adequate even for our own period in which art has far more autonomy—that poetic technique is developed entirely for its own sake out of a disinterested aesthetic concern for form and apart from both personal interests and the general interests of culture as a whole."[26] That is, all the traditional categories are not problematized as to their very logic, but are simply historicized as being perhaps more relevant to some periods than to others; and of course, the question of history itself is not problematized either.

As I have indicated, I think that it is precisely this conceptual complication which motivates Greenblatt's effort, but which he nevertheless fails to articulate as such. It seems to me that

Greenblatt's insufficient procedure depends on his desire to expose literature in the name of a political *context* which is revealed as its hidden truth, and that it is the thought of context which still dominates his thinking. And yet an indication of some other thought that complicates the very notion of context is hinted at, but not developed. Thus Greenblatt says: "A court lyric, to be sure, *may be considered apart from its creator and its immediate context:* it finds its way into commonplace books, is set to music . . . And after all, we know little enough about the precise circumstances of these poems, many of which have *come to us without clear attribution,* since appearance in print was something courtiers actively avoided. But if we grasp *the extent to which Wyatt and others like him were defined by their relations to power,* the extent to which they were at once attracted and repelled by Henry VIII and the world he represented, we grasp more readily in their poetry the heightened awareness of techniques of self-presentation and concealment."[27]

For Greenblatt, the understanding of political power as the motivation behind Wyatt's poetry depends on the importance of the category of context. Political power, or power as political, is the thought of context, and of the submission of the poem to the judgment of this court of context. *But isn't there a thinking that exceeds the thinking of context?* For it is perhaps, I suggest, rather precisely the thought of that which, in Greenblatt's terms, comes to us without clear attribution, and out of context, wherein a more complex possibility for thinking literature and the relations between the discourses might be found. It is this dimension of the poem which is perhaps the most remarkable as Greenblatt, it seems to me, actually senses, and more so in his later writings. For coming to us without clear attribution the poem suddenly reveals a dimension that isn't dependent on an external authority, political or otherwise, and the enigma of an utterance that can only speak with its own "authority" is disclosed. An utterance whose paternity, and therefore its established meaning, *cannot be known* as established from the outside, but rather, on some level, can only be received as event through a participation in its occurrence. This contextless authority involves the question of power as well, yet this question originates not from the stability of the context of political power, but rather from the promise of a dimension of thinking different from that of knowledge.[28]

These are therefore the main questions that seem to me to be raised by the problem which we can perhaps still call literature, and these are some of these issues that I try to examine and develop through a reading of the textual event, usually designated by the authorities of literary criticism as a novel, which is Herman Melville's *Moby-Dick*.

AMERICA—A WITNESSING OF EUROPE

Why, then, *Moby-Dick*? Why approach a nineteenth-century American text to investigate these issues that seem so closely tied to the problem of literature in the wake of the crisis of European identity, which has been increasingly evident since the second half of the nineteenth century,[29] and in the wake of the European disasters and catastrophes of the twentieth century and of the disasters brought forth in the name of "Europe" and its ideals?

It seems to me that *Moby-Dick* should occupy a central and exemplary place in such an investigation for many reasons, three of which are particularly important. First, there is what could be called the text's scene of utterance. *Moby-Dick* is presented as the testimony of one Ishmael, a survivor to a terrible disaster at sea, for which there are no other witnesses. Here the problem of the literary text is allegorically presented as the problem of an utterance, an utterance telling of a disaster, an utterance that can have no external guarantee, no external authority, other than its actual taking place. We therefore *cannot know* whether the testimony itself has the character of a fictional account or whether it is a true testimony to a disaster. In a way, this whole book is an attempt to work out the "logic" of this problem.

Second, *Moby-Dick* is exemplary for my investigations because its reception history has been marked by readers troubled by the instability of the text, its uncategorizability. Indeed, it has been quite impossible to decide what kind of text it is, whether a fictional story or a real testimony to a disaster. Thus one of the first reviewers of the book, Melville's friend Evert Duyckink, writes in 1851: "A difficulty in the estimate of this, in common with one or two other of Mr. Melville's books, occurs from the double character under which they present themselves. In one light they are romantic fictions, in another statements of absolute fact . . . It becomes quite impossible to submit such books to a distinct classification as fact, fiction, or essay."

It was thus felt from very early on that what is so disturbing about *Moby-Dick is precisely its excess as text over any simple understanding of its status as literature*. It opened the question of literature as that which is beyond or in excess of literature, at least as it was traditionally understood.

The third and most elaborate reason that I focus on *Moby-Dick* has to do with the *wounding strangeness* that the event, or series of events, called American literature, especially in its nineteenth century manifestations, has marked in relation to the European literary tradition and its conception of what literature is and could be; *Moby-Dick*, which is the story of a wounding strangeness called "the whale," can be said to occupy a strategic place in any attempt to define this strangeness. "There is a new feeling in the old American books," writes D. H. Lawrence, recognizing a certain rupture in the history of European letters ". . . There is a 'different' feeling in the old American classics. It is the shifting over from the old psyche to something new, a displacement. And displacements hurt. This hurts. So we try to tie it up, like a cut finger. Put a rag round it. It is a cut too. Cutting away the old emotions and consciousness. Don't ask what is left."[30] And Lawrence also writes: "There is an unthinkable gulf between us and America" and across this gulf "we see, not our own folk signalling to us, but strangers, incomprehensible beings, simulacra, perhaps of ourselves, but *other*, creatures from an other-world. The connection [between Europe and America] holds good historically for the past. In the pure present and in futurity it is not valid. The present reality is a reality of untranslatable otherness . . ."[31]

This incomprehensibility, this cutting wound that American literature inflicts, seems to imply that America as envisioned by Lawrence is not simply a geographical and historical place, but the raising anew of literature as a problem under the sign of something, a certain strangeness, which can be called "America." The phrase "American literature" in Lawrence's title should therefore not be understood as simply designating a literature written in America, but rather as Literature put into question, we might say *accused*, by something called "America." But this "America," Lawrence's book seems to say, is something which can *only* be heard "within" or *as* literature, in the textual events of Melville, Hawthorne, Poe, and the other writers to whom Lawrence responds, and it involves an accusation of America itself. "America," like literature for Artaud, is in excess of itself.

And what is witnessed as this "America" is, at one and the same time, a certain disaster—a disaster and destruction of something which Lawrence calls "Europe"—and a certain promise for a renewal of life and for a revolution in our existence, a revolution that also implies for Lawrence a new thinking of the political yet to come: "The real American day hasn't begun yet. Or at least not yet sunrise . . . Democracy in *America is just the tool with which the old master of Europe, the European spirit, is undermined. Europe destroyed*, potentially, American democracy will evaporate. America will begin."[32]

I thus suggest that "America" for Lawrence—and, I wish to add in passing, for Stanley Cavell, whose understanding of America is crucial in this context[33]—is something very close to what "theatre" is for Artaud, and that it is the performing of "America" which is at stake in his very theatrical book.[34]

"America" for Lawrence, we have seen, is the name for an event that announces, or even allows the witnessing of, the destruction of Europe.[35] Elaborating on this idea I would suggest that if indeed there is something particularly strange, even prophetic in feeling, thinking, and tone, in some nineteenth-century "American" works,[36] it might be because, paradoxically, it had witnessed or experienced the destruction of Europe in some way before Europe itself did. And *Moby-Dick*, a text dealing with the witnessing to a disaster and destruction by something called "the whale," can perhaps be said to be the text that meditates most profoundly on this event of destruction which we can call "America" and might be said to constitute *avant la lettre* a testimony to horrors which we have learned to associate with twentieth-century Europe.

Indeed, the destiny of *Moby-Dick* and the attempt to define what is at stake in this event or series of events which we can call

American literature were always closely tied, and this from two perspectives: 1) from Melville's self-definition, famously given expression in his essay "Hawthorne and his Mosses," in which he sets the task for the coming literature and calls for the liberation of American literature from European writing and its preeminent figure, Shakespeare. He thus defines American literature as a writing against Europe: "No American writer should write like an Englishman, or a Frenchman . . . Let us away with this literary flunkyism towards England . . . Let us boldly contemn all imitation . . . and foster all originality, though at first, it be crabbed and ugly as our own pine knots. And if any of our authors fail, or seem to fail, then, in the words of my enthusiastic Carolina cousin, let us clap him on the shoulder, and back him *against all Europe* for his second round."[37]

2) From the perspectives of the more scholarly attempt to come to terms with the question of American literature. A recent critical guide to *Moby-Dick* puts it in the following way: "The struggle to define *Moby-Dick* witnesses America's own struggles, as a new nation, to name and define the terms of its own culture. *Moby-Dick* is therefore a vital document, so to speak, in an American declaration of cultural independence. All the essays in this Critical Guide show how a reading of *Moby-Dick* has been used to plot the co-ordinates in a reading of America. *Moby-Dick* has thus been seen as *the* key text in the growth, development and reassessment of American studies."[38]

Partially accepting this description I would nevertheless inflect differently this exemplarity of *Moby-Dick* and its relation to the question of America, seeing it not so much as the key text to some independent cultural identity called America but rather as a key witness—which is, necessarily, as I have argued, a literary witness—to an event that is the destruction of the identity called

Europe and a revolutionary promise for something yet to come, an event which we might name "America."

It is the whale, I have begun to suggest, that is Melville's main figure for this destructive and revolutionary event with which I have associated, following Artaud, the name "theatre" and, with Lawrence, the name "America," and it is the act of witnessing this event and creating a witness of this event, that interests Melville. It is the encounter with the whale—I suggest here and develop further on—that involves the unmasterable excess I have specified as calling for the literary, or theatrical, witness, and we might say it is the whale that can be witnessed only "within" or *as* literature or theatre. The whale is therefore the figure around which my reading of *Moby-Dick* revolves and it is to its nature as event that I try to respond.

Yet the response that an event demands is, I have started to indicate, a witnessing/participation in the event, and it is this kind of *participation* in—which is not a communion with—the textual event *Moby-Dick*, that I try to achieve and can be said to constitute my way or "method" of reading. I therefore try to avoid as much as possible, in a way which might strike some as arbitrary or as anachronistically formalistic, any relation either to literary texts other than *Moby-Dick*, or its historical context, or "external" conceptual authorities that wish to dictate in advance what a text might or might not mean.[39]

I do this not because I view these questions as irrelevant or think that the text is autonomous and exclusively and sovereignly controls its own meaning. Rather, I do this from the opposite impression, that the text as event is absolutely helpless, exposed, and vulnerable to being stifled by a too quick resort to other voices that might be construed as elucidating its meaning; that becoming a witness to its singular address demands absolute concentration; and with the conviction that only by managing to hear what happens "within" the text or *as* the text, by *becoming* the event of the text, can a new "logic" of thinking and feeling be developed from which the questions of history—as context or as something else—of the text's relation to other literary events and non-literary discourses, and of the birth of the concepts which might be called for by the text, can be asked anew.

In one of his powerful and enigmatic utterances, Antonin Artaud attempts performatively to restore the capacity for theatre, that is, the capacity to witness/perform the event of disaster, or what he also calls the cry, which he feels has been eliminated from our existence: "No one knows how to scream anymore in Europe, least of all, actors. In a hypnotic trance, they can no longer utter a cry."[40] Can it be that what is a stake in "American" literature, and in *Moby-Dick* with its destructive/revolutionary figure of the whale, is precisely *Europe's learning to cry, or the becoming theatre of Europe?*

Can *Moby-Dick* become for us the teacher of the cry and can we, through a participation in, and performance of, *Moby-Dick* or of "the whale," learn to become actors of the cry? This is what is attempted, and what is at stake, in this book.

"The great theatre of Oklahoma calls you! Today only and never again! If you miss your chance now you miss it for ever! If you think of your future you are one of us! Everyone is welcome! If you want to be an artist join our company! Our theatre can find employment for everyone, a place for everyone! If you decide on an engagement we congratulate you here and now! But hurry, so that you get in before midnight! At twelve o'clock the doors will be shut and never open again! Down with those who do not believe in us! Up, and to Clayton!" (Franz Kafka—*Amerika*).

1

The Enigma of Power

> A poem, being an instance of language, hence essentially dialogue, may be a letter in a bottle thrown out to the sea with the—surely not always strong—hope that it may somehow wash up somewhere, perhaps on a shoreline of the heart
> —Paul Celan

> On the second day, a sail drew near, nearer, and picked me up at last. It was the devious-cruising Rachel, that in her retracing search after her missing children, only found another orphan
> —Herman Melville, the epilogue to *Moby-Dick*

Let us then move closer to *Moby-Dick* and start to examine the questions I have raised above from the perspective of the concrete encounter with a work of literature.

What happens between (or even in-between) a literary work and its readers? How can we even start to find a language, a way of thinking and feeling, with which to respond to this mysterious encounter? I propose to let Freud, who was himself troubled by these questions, serve as our tuning fork for the investigations to follow.

"Works of art," says Freud, "exercise a *powerful effect* on me, especially those of literature and sculpture, less often of painting. This has occasioned me, when I have been contemplating such things, to spend a long time before them, trying to apprehend them in my own way, i.e. to *explain* to myself what their effect is due to . . . Some rationalistic, or perhaps analytic turn of mind in me rebels against *being moved* by a thing *without knowing why I am thus affected* and what it is that affects me. This has brought me to recognize the apparently paradoxical fact that precisely some of the *grandest and overwhelming creations* of art are still *unsolved riddles* to our *understanding*. We admire them, we feel overawed by them, but we are *unable to say* what they represent to us."[1]

We can see that for Freud *something happens* when he encounters works of literature and art, something that involves the following: 1) Freud undergoes a certain overwhelming experience which he defines as his being powerfully affected. 2) This experience presents itself as a riddle, a question to be answered. 3) This experience causes speech, understanding and knowledge to collapse. An ability to speak and to know reaches a limit. Freud becomes helpless in front of the work. 4) Yet this encounter, precisely because it involves a collapse of speech, is simultaneously a call, or even an imperative, for a reinstatement of meaning and a restoration of speech, a call for interpretation: "*I must find out the meaning* and content of what is represented in the work; I must, in other words, *be able to interpret* it."[2]

While these ways of raising the question of the encounter with works of art and literature may be tied essentially to psychoanalysis, they are by no means exclusive to it, since they come from the nature of the works of art themselves. As an indication of this, let us take a look at a similar investigation, undertaken this time within a work of literature, by another rational and analytic, though pre-Freudian, investigator: Ishmael, the narrator of *Moby-Dick*. Trying to come to grips with the enigmatic question, the riddle, of the white whale and its powerful effect, Ishmael says: "What the white whale was to Ahab, has been hinted; what, at times, he was to me, as yet remains unsaid. Aside from those more obvious considerations touching Moby Dick, which could not but occasionally awaken in any man's soul some alarm, there was another thought, or rather vague, *nameless* horror, concerning him, which at times *by its intensity, completely overpowered* all the rest; and yet so mystical and well *nigh ineffable* was it, that I almost despair in putting it in comprehensible form. It was the whiteness of the whale that above all things appalled me. But how can I hope to explain myself here; and yet, in some dim, random way, *explain myself I must*, else all these chapters might be naught" (p. 188). And a few pages later: "But not yet have we *solved* the incantation of this whiteness, and learned why it *appeals with such power to the soul*" (p. 195).[3]

A structure of issues, quite similar to Freud's, suggests itself, this time in relation to the whiteness of the whale: 1) It has a powerful effect on Ishmael. 2) This effect presents itself as a riddle, as an enigmatic question. 3) This experience of whiteness takes shape as a collapse of speech, a limit that is called ineffability, or namelessness, is here reached. Ishmael becomes helpless. 4) Nevertheless, this collapse is here again a call, or an imperative demand for explanation and interpretation, for a restoration of speech.

Thus through Freud's discussion of the work of literature and Ishmael's discussion of the white whale (we have yet to determine how it might be related to the encounter with a work of literature) a certain *structure of an encounter* is revealed. This structure brings together the following points, demands that they be thought together: a) a certain event takes place in language or happens to language and causes it to collapse, to reach a limit; this event is also characterized by a collapse of knowledge and of understanding. b) This event calls for a certain vocabulary that we might term a *vocabulary of power*. An attempt to say this limit-dimension of language demands that we use this vocabulary of power, which for Freud involves the expression of being moved and being affected, and for Ishmael raises the question of the soul. c) The linguistic form most associated with this event is the riddle or the enigma. This event is experienced as an enigma. d) This event signals the place or the moment in which and from which language is most crucially called for, demanded, in which it perhaps originates.

Taking this line of thinking somewhat further, we might say that e) the form in which language arrives, or at least one of its major configurations as called for by this powerful riddle, might be that of the question of literature, understood in this context as the question of the event of its encounter. We might even say that the encounter itself, the powerful riddle that it is, is but the raising of the question of its own enigma; the event of the encounter *is* this question. (This does not mean that this question has an answer or can be resolved.) Thus the question about the encounter with the literary work is not exterior to the event of its taking place, does not come from a discourse exterior to literature that subjects it to its own modes of questioning and authority (be it psychoanalysis or philosophy), but rather is its taking place. Of course we do not yet know what this might mean and what it involves. We can perhaps say that *what questions in us, through us, is the event questioning itself.*

It is from within the space of questioning opened up by these structural relations, concentrating on the importance they give to the vocabulary of power, that I propose to investigate the question of the encounter with a work of literature through the reading of the enigmatic textual event called *Moby-Dick*.

Indeed, the description of the encounter with *Moby-Dick* as having a powerful effect has been expressed by many of this book's commentators. We can take as a representative response the following words by Alfred Kazin: "It is this constant sense of power that constitutes the book's appeal to us, that explains its hold on our attention . . . If we start by opening ourselves to this abundance and force, by welcoming not merely the story itself, but the manner in which it speaks to us, we shall recognize in this restlessness, this richness, this persistent atmosphere of magnitude, the essential image on which the book is founded."[4]

But, interestingly enough, the vocabulary of power used so often when discussing *Moby-Dick* is not restricted to a description of the reading *experience*; it comes up in almost any attempt to *interpret* the novel, to uncover its *meaning*.

The vocabulary of power is most apt to appear in political interpretations of the novel, readings that usually regard the relations between the narrator-survivor Ishmael and the mad, tyrannical Captain Ahab as the axis along which an allegory of the uses and abuses of political power can be deciphered. Let us take as an example one such politically-oriented critic. The (New-Americanist) critic Donald Pease, commenting on a group that he terms the Cold War critics, writes: "Ever since Mathiessen's reading of [*Moby-Dick*] as the sign of the power of the freedom of figures in the American Renaissance to oppose totalitarianism, *Moby-Dick* has been a Cold War text, one that secures in Ishmael's survival a sign of the *free world's triumph over a totalitarian power*."[5]

In this reading, a tradition of critics regarded *Moby-Dick* as dramatizing a successful fight against a totalitarian, political, power represented by Ahab. For Pease, this is a faulty political interpretation of the novel, since he recognizes another center of power besides Ahab, and that is Ishmael himself. According to this interpretation Ishmael represents a power that is politically not less dangerous than Ahab's totalitarianism, a persuasive, rhetorical power: "Ishmael uncouples the actions that occur from the motives giving rise to them, thereby turning virtually all events in the narrative into an opportunity to display the powers of eloquence capable of taking possession of them. Indeed nothing, and *no one resists Ishmael's power* to convert the world he sees into the forms of rhetoric that he wants."[6] Pease sees Ahab's and Ishmael's powers as complicit and suggests that the novel might still be about resistance to oppressive powers. Melville, he writes, "works through the vicious circulation informing the conflicted will at work in Ishmael and Ahab. If the Cold War consensus would turn *Moby-Dick* into a figure through which it could read the free world's survival in the future struggle with totalitarianism, Melville, as it were, speaks back through the same figure, asking us if we could survive the free world that Ishmael has handed down to us."[7] Thus the novel for Pease is still about crucial political resistance to power, only power is no longer located exclusively in Ahab but also in Ishmael.

A third significant context permeated by the vocabulary of power does not have to do with the experience of the novel or with its interpretation, but rather concerns itself with the place *Moby-Dick* occupies in Melville's oeuvre and life. It is almost a commonplace of Melville criticism that with *Moby-Dick* Melville reached the height of his creative powers and thereafter declined, losing power and creative strength before falling almost completely silent for forty years, until the semi-recovery of power in his late, posthumously published novel *Billy Budd*.[8]

I could give more examples of interpretations that resort to using the vocabulary of power, in many different modalities that encompass more than just the political. Usually power, mostly in its political modality, is evaluated as oppressive and demanding resistance, a critique. Less often, as is the case in Kazin, power is celebrated—after all, *Moby-Dick* is known as "our mighty book." Yet the multiplication of such examples is not essential for the following discussions. What is essential to these diverse examples are the following points: 1) although the vocabulary of power, like the white whale of the sailors' myths, is ubiquitous in Melville criticism, the question has never been raised whether these multiple and different occasions and modalities of resorting to the vocabulary of power are simply nominal coincidences, that is, simply coincidences of resorting to a similar vocabulary, to the same words, or whether there is indeed a common question which all these occasions point to and from which they derive.[9]

2) If there were a common question behind these coincidences of vocabulary, I would argue that this has something to do with the vocabulary of power used by the novel itself, to which the critics, in many different ways, respond. But it is precisely these two points that most, if not all, critics seem to ignore. This apparent oversight has two consequences. That the vocabulary of power is so pervasive in the novel itself has not signaled to the critics that power in Moby-Dick is not a mythical self-explanatory entity falling from the sky. The critical attention has not been directed towards this vocabulary itself as one that might be problematized and investigated by the novel. The possibility has not been raised that the novel does not simply accept the mean-

ing of power as self-evident, but is rather searching for the realm that demands its use and makes it necessary to resort to this specific vocabulary.

It is precisely because this latter question has not been raised that the vocabulary of power used by the critics has not itself been put into question, but has been employed as if its meanings were self-explanatory. Thus the repetition of the vocabulary of the novel in the criticism was not problematized or understood otherwise than as a simple referral, an unproblematic one-to-one correspondence between the language of the novel and the language of criticism. Consequently, the only critical problem was to decide who is in possession of power in the novel, and whether this should be interpreted as good or bad. The status of the critical *response*, in other words, was never put into question; it was never suspected that there is something about the questioning of the vocabulary of power performed by the novel that is at the source of its demand for a critical response; or, going even further, that the very notion of critical response in general might be in some essential way related to an investigation of the vocabulary of power.

Let us then face the text.

Since the question of encounter with a specific linguistic event, usually referred to as literary, is at the center of my attention in this book, let us begin our reading of *Moby-Dick* by examining the way it *frames* its own event, stages its own encounter; that is, the way in which in the most general manner it *addresses* the reader. What kind of address is involved in this "novel"? How is the reader positioned in relation to it?

2

Call Me Ishmael

In the great tradition of sea narratives, *Moby-Dick* is a story told by a returning sailor, Ishmael, the sole survivor of a terrible disaster at sea caused by a great and fabulous monster, the white leviathan Moby-Dick. As if to convince a hesitant crowd, of whose interest in the tale he is not quite confident, this Ishmael calls upon his readers to pay attention, to call him Ishmael and to listen to his tale. He comes from an important and eminent family (of course, who doesn't in such stories?). He is an instructor, a teacher of the young, and hence an all-around trustworthy fellow whose story should definitely be heeded. His story begins in the following manner: He was bored, nearly wanted to kill himself! And thus, instead of doing that, he decided without much further ado to go to sea. The devil knows why, he decided to go a-whaling, it could not have been his choice, it must have been some great force, fate, that persuaded him to do so. And thus, with a couple of cents in his pocket, ready for any adventure his good fortune was preparing for him, he was off on his way.

But perhaps we should start again?

Moby-Dick is the narrative of Ishmael, the single survivor and sole witness to a horrendous disaster at sea in which all his friends were killed and brought to an early, stoneless and unmarked grave. As if wanting to share in his friends' destiny, he has left his given name at sea and has adopted the Biblical name Ishmael, thus indicating his abandonment and loss. From now on he wishes to be called Ishmael and not by his given name, which remains forever unknown. The story we are about to hear is his testimony, and it is a testimony of a survivor.

He was a schoolteacher, passing on knowledge to the next generation. He was on occasion the victim of suicidal depressions and anxiety. But instead of committing suicide, he would go on a sea voyage as a sailor. On the occasion that has prompted the testimony we are about to hear, he decided to go on a whaling voyage. He could not say exactly why: there was something powerful about the whale that attracted him—and he accepted this power as a call of destiny that chose him, perhaps to be a survivor and to tell the stories of those who were not so fortunate, to speak as they could not. He thus took his humble belongings and went to sea.

What, then, is the form of address of this novel that so famously opens by, precisely, addressing the reader? Is the reader called to listen to the tale of a fabulous sea voyage, to a seaman's fantastic and ludicrously exaggerated yarn of incredible adventures and unbelievable monsters (as the first version demonstrates)? Or is the reader called upon to listen to a grave narrative of testimony to a disaster, to a surviving teacher's moving words that bear witness to the limits of existence (as the second version demonstrates)?[1] It is precisely this splitting of the form of address, this capacity for simultaneous listening called for by the novel, that seems to me to constitute Melville's greatest achievement in *Moby-Dick*. I argue that it is precisely by trying to follow the implications of this double form of address that we will be able to understand what the novel has to teach us about the question of the literary encounter. The encounter with literary language, the novel seems to suggest, is a confrontation with a language whose singularity has to do with its being a fabulous or fictional language and, simultaneously, a testimonial language to a disaster.

But how could these two come together at the same time, since fiction and testimony seem in the most commonsensical way to oppose each other?[2] If the one has to do with invention, imagination, and even with lying, the other has to do with historical truth, referentiality, and with actual and real events.[3] Needless to say, the novel itself is acutely aware of this fundamental ambiguity of its language and constantly raises the issue of this ambiguity, and from many perspectives. Here is one such example, spoken by Ishmael, this time as a messenger of referential truth: "I do not know where I can find a better place than just here, to make mention of one or two other things, which to me seem important, as in printed form establishing in all respects the reasonableness of the whole story of the White Whale, more especially the *catastrophe*. For this is one of those disheartening instances where *truth* requires full as much bolstering as error. So ignorant are most landsmen of some of the plainest and most palpable wonders of the world, that without some hint touching the plain facts, historical and otherwise, of the fishery, they might scout at Moby Dick as a *monstrous fable*, or still worse and more detestable, a hideous and intolerable allegory." And three paragraphs later, he notes: " But fortunately the special point I here seek can be established upon *testimony* entirely independent of my own" (pp. 205–6).

Let us then begin to unravel the various implications involved in this novel's complex and ambiguous structure of address by retracing our steps and examining more closely this dual framing of the novel. *Moby-Dick*, then, is either a story told by a returning sailor whose name is or isn't Ishmael, and who is or isn't a former schoolteacher, who tells a marvelous, fictional, and fabulous story the aim of which is either to persuade the listeners of its fantastical veracity or simply to delight and please them with a deliberately exaggerated and fictional language whose epistemic value as either true or false is secondary to the demonstration of its sheer power of invention. Or, *Moby-Dick* is true testimony of a survivor, a returning sailor, formerly a schoolteacher, whose name Ishmael is either his given name, or, more likely, a symbolic name taken as a gesture of identification with his lost comrades, and chosen for its biblical connotations of banishment and abandonment.[4]

Ishmael's story might aim both to persuade his readers that disasters such as these, monstrous as they may sound, are possible and in fact have actually happened, and to make the readers themselves further witnesses to the disaster, carrying this horrific story with them into the future, reverberating it, and assuring that it will not be forgotten—but also mourning together a certain past that was never experienced. It might also be that the sailor, like Coleridge's Ancient Mariner (explicitly alluded to in the novel), cannot bear alone this traumatic event and has to share it with others simply in order to be able to go on living, as if his survival does not simply depend on his actual physical rescue but requires a different kind of achievement, which is that of the power to live through the telling of one's story.[5]

We may see how some of these possibilities come together around the multiple ways we can read the famous opening, "Call me Ishmael." This opening thus says: either my name is Ishmael and you should call me by my name; or this is not my given name, but one called for by the conventions of fiction; or it is my symbolic name, carefully chosen, and in order to explain why I chose it I have to tell you my life's story; or, since I am an abandoned human, and feel like a disowned son, I call upon you, the readers, to adopt me and call me by this name so that I won't be alone anymore.[6]

By thus unfurling several of the various possibilities generated by the novel's structure of address, we are faced with the following issues and questions. 1) This complex address seems to *exclude any final and unified meaning* to be assigned to the novel through a process of interpretation. Any such meaning could right away be fed into this vortex formed by the undecidability between the fabulous and the testimonial and would be decomposed again into several incommensurable possibilities, into the structure of the either/or.

2) The very fact that this impossibility of unified meaning has to do with a complex structure of address—understood first and foremost in relation to a call (call me Ishmael?)—seems to suggest, and we will have to examine this suggestion, that *there is something in the very notion of address, or of the call, which goes beyond, or is in excess of, the notion of meaning*, or at least of unified meaning. It is as if the question of, and the quest for, meaning is generated by this address, by this call, but the address is irreducible to its products. Or putting it differently, it is as if language is first of all an address and only secondarily a statement of meaning, and this address is always produced by a dynamic that goes beyond any static, stated meanings.

3) This overflowing of unified meaning by the structure of the address or the call brings about a *change of emphasis from the*

question of meaning to the question of authority and power, or rather to the question of authority and power over meaning.[8] A decision of meaning is discovered to involve implicitly a decision about what authority presides over meaning, an unconscious implication that is discovered only when the jurisdiction of one authority seems to be contested by that of another. We thus no longer ask: what does the text mean? But, rather, what is the competing structure of authorities or of forces that prevents the text from being assembled into a unified meaning? Since it is precisely because it is no longer clear who has authority in the text, who holds the key to its decoding, that it is impossible to reach a stable meaning. The reader, destabilized and perplexed, does not know *as who* he/she is addressed. Is the authority presiding over the text the one of truth and the referentiality of actual events—the authority, for example, that ideally belongs to the legal witness?[9] Or, is the authority the one given to the fabulist, the authority to use language not mainly in relation to truth or falsity but, for example, as a sheer inventive luxury meant to astonish?

This change of emphasis suggests that an investigation into the literary encounter is necessarily an inquiry into the question of authority. If, as I have begun to suggest, the question of authority opens up and discloses itself in the irreducible difference between the linguistic address and linguistic meaning, we would have to ask what precisely are the relations between the question of address and the question of authority. What, exactly, is an address, and what exactly is authority? Is the address itself a structure of authority, or is authority a certain way to arrest the whirlwind of meanings that the address unleashes, a certain way to quiet and stabilize the revolution brought forth by the address by demarcating what is for referential truth and what for fiction?

And if so, who takes authority to take authority, and by what right; who, or what, if anything, authorizes someone to decide for truth or for fabulation, among others?[10]

4) Since it is precisely in the space between the language of testimony to a disaster and a fabulous, fictional, language that this problematics of the address and of authority arises, our efforts will concentrate on thinking together the relations among the following terms: a testimonial language; a fabulous, fictional language; the question of linguistic address; the question of authority; and the question of meaning. Why is it that these have to be thought together if we are to understand the literary encounter? This seems to me to be the central question suggested by the novel, and one that will guide the following discussions. All this in the attempt to answer our initial question—why is it that the encounter with the singular language of literature calls for recourse to a vocabulary of power and the collapse of the vocabulary of knowledge?

These issues and questions, which we have discovered through an analysis of the novel's framing device, are, of course, not restricted to it. Rather, they might be said to govern the whole narrative logic and thematic development of the novel. Let us then briefly outline the novel's trajectory: In lieu of committing suicide, the melancholy "schoolmaster"/narrator Ishmael decides to temporarily abandon his stable life on land and take off toward unknown destinations and adventures at sea. He is struck by the overwhelming idea of the whale and decides to enlist in the crew of a whaling ship. Before he ships out to sea, on a journey narrated at some length, Ishmael has an initially shocking encounter with the tattooed stranger Queequeg, but shortly thereafter the two become close friends.

Queequeg is a savage prince, son of the king of the fabulous and unknown island Kokovoko, who has set off to learn the ways of the world so that he can return to instruct his countrymen. Queequeg's quest for Western knowledge results in his corruption, whereby he is no longer entitled to return and rule his people until his spiritual purification, and he therefore spends his time whaling. Ishmael and Queequeg discover that they both intend to embark on a whaling voyage; and on the following day, looking for a ship which can accommodate both of them, Ishmael hits upon what seems to him the right one, the *Pequod*, and together the two friends set sail.

Broadly speaking, from the moment the novel sets off to sea, as it were, Ishmael's narration takes on a double focus: first there is the actual story, told chronologically, of the *Pequod*'s voyage to hunt the sperm whale. In general, the mission of sperm-whale hunts is an economic one—to kill as many whales as possible in order to extract oil from their blubber, oil that will be used to light up the dark nights of the inhabitants of the land. Yet this specific voyage is dominated by the ship's commander Captain Ahab's obsession with hunting one whale, the White Whale Moby Dick, who has terribly wounded and mutilated him in their previous encounter.

This Moby Dick is a legendary, semi-mythical creature, the subject of astonishing, fabulous sailor stories as well as personal testimonies by past victims to the disasters he has caused. Ahab's monomaniacal hunt for him reaches its apocalyptic conclusion in the terrible disaster of the ship's destruction by Moby Dick, wherein the whole crew of the *Pequod*, with the exception of Ishmael, are killed. As this story line progresses Ishmael practically disappears as a participant in the action, becoming a bodiless voice that testifies and comments on the events, explaining them and bringing them to us.

This main story line is constantly interrupted by, and suspended in favor of, the second focus of the narrative—the writer and whale-author Ishmael's lengthy meditations on whales. These meditations, which occupy many chapters and are supposedly the main incentive for his storytelling in the first place, are dedicated to exploring the question of the whale and its meaning. Ishmael's narration in these chapters is extremely varied and unstable and shifts constantly through several discourses—scientific, theological, autobiographical-testimonial, fabulous-mythical, etc.—all in an attempt to respond to the enigma that is the whale and the disaster of its encounter.

With the help of this schematic outline we can begin to delineate the major foci of the novel's articulation of the problems we have raised above. We might say that the novel's trajectory involves three movements, three voyages, which originate in *a crisis of authority*, a crisis in the stability of meaning. This crisis affects the three foci of authority in the novel. The first is the departing sailor Ishmael, the protagonist of the story, whose voyage is associated with a loss of authority—first, because of his abdication of his position as a schoolmaster—that is, the master of the meanings to be transmitted to the students; second, his naming himself Ishmael indicates an abandonment by the authority of the father and an exilic, homeless, existence in the lawless desert; and, finally, Ishmael refuses to take any position of authority on the ship: "nor do I ever go to sea as a Commodore, or a Captain, or a Cook. I abandon the glory and distinction of such offices to those who like them" (p. 5).[11] What comes together for Ishmael with this abdication of authority is the "overwhelming idea of the great whale" (p. 7), which draws him into a whaling voyage as a substitute for the authority on land which he had to abandon.

The second center of authority is the commander, Captain Ahab, whose enraged chase after Moby Dick originates in the terrible wound he suffered, a wound not, as we will see, simply physical, but a wound precisely to his authoritative position as captain. Ahab's chase problematizes authority on another level as well, and this in relation to the sailors and to their understanding of the nature of whale hunting in general. Because of his singular chase after Moby Dick, Ahab breaks the implicit law of whaling which demands that any whale whatsoever be hunted down. Ahab is not interested in just any whale, but in *this* singular whale, and thus, in a way, exceeds the very dictation of the law in whose name his authority as captain is given.[12]

The third focus of authority to be problematized in the novel is that of Ishmael as, precisely, a "whale *author*" (p. 456). As an aspiring author and an authority on whales, Ishmael's self-professed mission and starting point is to write the whale's "as yet . . . unwritten life" (p. 135), to attempt to solve for the first time the enigma that is the whale's existence. Ishmael takes this mission very seriously and attempts to exhaust from all its aspects the nature and meaning of the whale, to transform the whale into an entirely transparent and meaningful text: "Since I have undertaken to manhandle this Leviathan, it behoves me to approve myself *omnisciently exhaustive* in the enterprise; not overlooking the minutest seminal germs of his blood, and spinning him out to the uttermost coil of his bowels" (p. 455). But Ishmael's exhaustive efforts constantly fail, his whale-authority is never fully established, because it is in the nature of his theme, the whale, to resist systematization and a unified interpretation.[13]

If these three foci (in addition to the framing voice of the ambivalent story-teller Ishmael) indeed testify to a constant problematization of the question of authority in the novel, then what is common to all of them, that which can be said to constitute precisely their *decentering*, the impossibility of establishing once and for all their authority, is the whale. Whether as an actual wounding agent in the commander Ahab's case, or as an untotalizable and unstable theme for the whale-author Ishmael, or as an overwhelming idea in the mind of Ishmael the ordinary seaman, *the whale is almost invariably that which is associated in the novel with the crisis of authority; it is that which interrupts, which calls into question, any stabilizing attempt of authoritative mastery*.[14] Yet this instability of the whale, this ungraspable nature characterized throughout as a challenge to a unified authorial voice, has a structure quite similar to the one we have identified as the ambivalent structure of the novel's framing address.

In a manner similar to the double form of address of the novel—as fabulous tale and as testimony to a disaster, an ambivalence that we have identified as preventing any unified allocation of authority—the mode in which the whale interrupts authority seems precisely to be linked, in a way which we will have to understand, with the continual wavering of its status from the real agent of a terrible and disastrous event to a fabulous, semi-mythical and even supernatural creature, whose actual existence is less important than the rumors and stories it generates.

This is true both of the double status of Moby Dick, and of the wavering status of the whale-author Ishmael's theme, whose discourse about the elusive whale is forever shifting, encompassing scientific descriptions, autobiographical testimony, and theological, fabulous and mythical stories and speculations.[15] This seems to suggest that the novel is addressed to the reader as, precisely, a whale; and that it is as a whale that the novel raises the question of the authority of its own discourse, on the one hand, and the authority of the reader as the master of interpreted meanings on the other. But what does it mean to be addressed by a whale, what does such an address involve and what kind of response does it demand?

LEVIATHANALYSIS

I propose the following hypothesis: responding to these questions and thinking further about these issues raised by the novel involves us the readers, the presumed masters of interpreted meanings, in slowly undergoing a *transformation or even a revolution in our ways of thinking and in our ways of feeling*. It seems to me that the ambition of this whale-novel extends to nothing less than this revolution. The principle in whose name the novel attempts to bring about this revolution is, precisely, the authority-interrupting whale. I argue that the whale, for the novel, is not only one of the characters, nor does it simply bring forth a theme which the novel seeks to develop; rather, it is a demanding address and a call, and perhaps also a promise, for a new way of listening, thinking, and feeling, for a new way of asking questions, for a new way of investigation; in short, for a new way of reading.

What is crucial about this demanding address or call is that we do not know from where, and how, and even if, it is issued, and what at all it asks of us—and we also do not know because of the trembling status of the whale between the fabulous-fictional creature and the agent of a real disaster. How are we, then, to undergo this revolution that is issued, perhaps, in the name of such an enigmatic principle[16] and does not tell us what to do and how to act, that is, a revolution that is not issued by the text as a presumed master of conveyed meanings and a presumed judge of the just action?[17] It is partly to this strange question which the rest of this book is dedicated, and I propose that the kind of response called for by the novel and which I will try to sketch might be named a leviathanalysis, or an attempt at whale-thinking.

The whale, we have begun to see, is not a unified entity or meaning, but an event of address with a "logic" of its own (a glimpse of which has shown us it involves the interruption of authority), which adopts very different manifestations. Indeed, it seems that its logic depends on, and consists of, the fact that its manifestation is multiple and cannot be unified as meaning.[18] Undergoing leviathanalysis involves a conceptual elaboration inseparable from an emotional transformation. It will mean, to begin with and among other things, being slowly exposed to the various aspects of the manifestation of the address of the whale followed by an attempt to slowly think together these aspects in their difference and to understand exactly the nature of this logical unity which we, so far, can only sense.

Let us begin to undergo this leviathanalysis.

3

Ahab's Whale—A Bleeding Wound

We shall start with the encounter that might be said to constitute the heart of the novel's main narrative, the source of much of its driving energy and its shattering pathos. I am referring to the event of Ahab's first disastrous encounter with Moby Dick, wherein he was terribly wounded and dismembered, an encounter which is at the origin of Ahab's passionate and obsessive chase. What is the nature of this event of encounter? What happens within it, and what does it mean, what horizon of questions and issues does it open, that under one of its main aspects the address of the whale (and we will have to see why this encounter should indeed be termed an address) is the infliction of the suffering of a terrible bodily wound?

"It is not probable that this monomania in him [the monomania of hunting the whale] took its instant rise at the precise time of his bodily dismemberment. Then, in darting at the monster, knife in hand, he had but given loose to a sudden, passionate, corporal animosity; and when he received the stroke that tore him, he probably but felt the agonizing bodily laceration, but nothing more. Yet, when by this collision *forced* to turn towards home, and for long months of days and weeks, Ahab and anguish lay stretched together in one hammock, rounding in mid winter that dreary, howling Patagonian Cape; then it was, that his *torn body and gashed soul bled into one another; and so interfusing, made him mad.* . . . though unlimbed of a leg, yet such *vital strength* yet lurked in his Egyptian chest, and was moreover *intensified* by his delirium, that his mates were forced to lace him fast, even there, as he sailed, raving in his hammock" (pp. 184–85).

Understanding, in Ahab's case, what the address of a whale involves forces us, then, to think what the event of wounding means. Ahab's wound, as this passage suggests, is for him not just the actual and painful cutting open of the body, but is the more significant and painful realization that the body *can* be cut open, that the body is in principle an open wound, that is, a vulnerability and an exposure to the whales of the outside, of the open sea, which it does not master. This exposure of the body characterizes it first of all as *passivity*, and it is this passivity that Ahab discovers when he is *forced* to lay anguished and helpless in his hammock for months, subjected to the rocking waves.

For it is indeed the vocabulary of power that is called for by the event of being wounded and exposed to the whale, a vocabulary called for in this passage in two ways: 1) Ahab is forced to change his course, the sense and direction of his voyage. Thus we can see that *the vocabulary of power is called for when a dimension of meaning or sense is introduced into the suffering of the wound*, since the wound becomes more than a bodily wound, it becomes a crisis of Ahab's authority, a collapse and exhaustion of his mastery as a captain and a commander *to give sense*, to direct and be the master of his voyage's meaning. 2) But at the same time, this event of wounding also intensifies Ahab's vital strength, of the *power of his life*. As if life, far from being only the physical or biological fact of existence, is an intensity and a force with the character of an open wound, which is inflamed and intensified precisely by being exposed to external provocation.[1] It is in this sense that the wounding whale might be said to be, surprisingly, a provocative and inspiring call for life.

What happens, then, to this commander when he is forced to discover his passivity; that is, when he is *forced to discover the body* as wound to whose sense he is subjected, or the body as the impotence at the heart of his will and of his ideal mastery of meaning?[2] He goes mad. Which is to say, it is precisely the dimension of meaning or sense, which, as we have seen, was introduced into the event of wounding, that comes to the fore as a crisis and becomes the central issue. Ahab undergoes a crisis that is a maddening disorientation of his senses.

Let us look more closely at this relation that is at the center of Ahab's adventure, a relation between the dimension of meaning and his event of wounding that is articulated on the basis of Ahab's understanding of the whale. This understanding is given in the following passage:

> All visible objects, man, are but as pasteboard masks. But in each event—in the living act, the undoubted deed—there, some unknown but still reasoning thing puts forth the mouldings of its features behind the unreasonable mask. If man will strike, strike through the mask! How can the prisoner reach outside except by thrusting through the wall? To me, the white whale is that wall, shoved near to me. Sometimes I think there's naught beyond. But 'tis enough. He tasks me; he heaps me; I see in him *outrageous strength, with an inscrutable malice* sinewing it. That *inscrutable* thing is chiefly what I hate; and be the white whale agent, or be the white whale principal, I will wreak that hate upon him. (p. 164)

The unbelievable, shocking, and monstrous wounding encounter with the whale irrupts for Ahab as an inscrutable and enigmatic riddle: what does the whale mean? Like Freud in front of Michelangelo's *Moses*, Ahab must find out the meaning of this whale. For although he is incomprehensible, the wounding whale, Ahab feels, is precisely *addressed to him*, and, outrageously, like a prophetic Jonah (or Moses) he hides the secret meaning of his mysterious destiny and his unaccounted-for origin in unfathomable depths. Ahab is convinced that his event of wounding means something, that it is not an arbitrary tearing open of the body. *The bodily event of wounding becomes for Ahab*—and therein lays the source both of his greatness and of his madness—*a burning question of meaning, a riddle.*

As a consequence, the encounter with the whale brings together for Ahab what for everyone else are two unrelated elements: a bodily wounding, which the others interpret as an arbitrary, nasty, brutish, and short attack that doesn't mean a thing, and a signifying aspect that makes this attack full of meaning for him. Or otherwise put, the encounter with the whale has to do with an experience of a crisis of meaning where others see only insignificant arbitrariness. What the whale means is unknown, the event of its encounter is a surprising event where knowledge collapses, but it is almost certain to Ahab, and only to him (and he is therefore the only witness to this near-certainty) that it means something different than what it signifies to everyone else. This is precisely what Ahab's chief mate and opponent Starbuck understands as madness: "Vengeance on a dumb brute, that simply smote thee from the blindest instinct! Madness!" (pp. 163–64).

We might therefore suggest that what comes together for Ahab through long months of subjection as an exposed wounded body and his impotence in orienting the ship is the enigmatic relation between the two meanings of the word "sense." *Ahab's madness is the madness of sense and the madness of the confusion and infusion (or the bleeding)*[3] *between the two meanings of "sense":* that is, it is the madness of the transition and relation between the physical meaning of sense—the exposure of the tactile surfaces of the body to external provocation—and the meaning of sense as meaning, direction and orientation. What is the relation between these two meanings of sense, what is the relation between the living body as passive surfaces of sensitivity that can be wounded and the body that speaks, that uses language or perhaps is used by language, to convey meanings and give orientation? This might be the enigma at the very heart of the novel, and on some level all our following discussions will revolve around it.

Thus the whale as address, in Ahab's case, is that which opens up this enigmatic and inscrutable in-between of the two meanings of sense. It is precisely here that its inscrutability lies, and it is precisely in this that it also means differently than any other reasonable thing which is meaningful to everyone and can be reduced to knowledge.[4] But not only is the whale inscrutable, it is also outrageously powerful, and this secretive and enigmatic inscrutability of the whale calls for a vocabulary of power here as well—in this case to address the whale's strength. The vocabulary of power is called for here not to designate the whale's strength in its capacity to overpower Ahab; neither is it called for to describe its physical force as a capacity to destroy and wound. Rather, it is called for precisely by the experience of the enigmatic relation, and of the gap, between the sensitive exposure of the wounded skin and the inscription of sense or meaning which seems discernible in this wound as an addressed letter left as a scar.[5]

This enigma of the whale, which makes Ahab suspect a hidden meaning where there seems to be only a simple wound,[6] is also why the whale personifies Evil and the demonic to Ahab, and it is also what raises the question of allegory in relation to this whale-novel:[7] "Evil as such. . . . ," writes Walter Benjamin, "exists only as allegory, is nothing other than allegory, and means something different from what it is. It means precisely the non-existence of what it presents."[8]

What is it that comes out of Ahab's exposure to the addressed and wounding letter, which is the whale Moby Dick?[9] What irrupts on this boundary between the wound and meaning? A drive. From now on Ahab's adventure is dictated by a *drive to hunt* and a *desire* beyond his control: "For with little external to constrain us, the innermost necessities in our being, these still *drive us on*" (p. 165). Ahab's forced course, which eventually leads to his death, is set as an unstoppable machine: "The path to my fixed purpose is laid with iron rails, whereon my soul is grooved to run. Over unsounded gorges, through the rifled hearts of mountains, under torrents' beds, unerringly I rush! Naught's an obstacle, naught's an angle to the iron way" (p. 168).[10]

As a conclusion to this discussion we might suggest that the enigma of the human, as the novel presents it through Ahab, asserts itself in one of its aspects as that of an animal, a creature involved in a simultaneous opening and a mysterious interdependence between a weak and fragile body, infinitely sensitive and vulnerable to being wounded by the slightest force to which it is exposed,[11] and an enormous power that can signify and assign through language meanings to these forces and can direct itself and give these forces directions; this ability seems precisely to involve the folding back upon itself of this vulnerability, which thus becomes an instrument of power and mastery. The drive, for the novel, originates as a *marking* on the sensitive body that has already been experienced as a *directive*, i.e. on the limit of meaning, yet remains undecipherable and incomprehensible; neither physical body nor spiritual meaning, but the gap between them.[12] The address of the whale, in Ahab's case, is thus that which reveals, calls for, creates, and comes to occupy the enigmatic and "inhuman" place of the drive. It is also that which marks the limit of the manipulation involved in the signifying language of the commander.

Language as Hunt; Language as Wail

Let us now direct our attention more closely to the question of language in Ahab's case. We have seen that the wounding address of the whale is not simply a question of a wound to the body but to a *certain* relation to language as well. It is the collapse of the understanding of language as the language of a commander, or of a sovereign and king,[13] which involves an ideal mastery of stable meanings to be used at will whereby any meaningful utterance is guaranteed the execution of its posited action. What happens then to Ahab's language after such a wounding event? What becomes of a language that has lost its stable grounding in meaning, when it has lost its anchorage point, and has found itself exposed to the immensities and rhythms of the rocking waves of the sea and to the address of whales? Or, in more conceptual terms, what implications will the disclosure of the relations among the body as wound, the drive, and the address of the whale have for the question of language?

I will approach this question from two perspectives. 1) By examining how the mad and wounded Ahab *uses and manipulates* language following his accident. 2) By examining how this wounded language nevertheless *speaks through* Ahab as a different kind of language, and how a call to understand language and meaning differently can be heard in his utterances and exceeds their control.

Mad Ahab's use of language is completely absorbed and possessed by the drive which controls him with its sole aim, the *hunt* and capture of the whale Moby Dick who has so terribly wounded him. His every utterance is consumed by this absolute and infinite desire (which is also a desire for the Infinite and the Absolute[14]) and everything and everyone are viewed as instruments he needs to control to fulfill his desire. His drive to hunt therefore becomes a *drive for mastery;* his language, the *language of tyranny and terror.* In a way he says nothing else but "Moby Dick," his language becomes nothing but "a whale": "Though, consumed with the hot fire of his purpose, Ahab in all his thoughts and actions ever had in view the ultimate capture of Moby Dick; though he seemed ready to sacrifice all mortal interests to that *one* passion . . . *To accomplish his object Ahab must use tools*; and of all tools used in the shadow of the moon, men are most apt to get out of order" (p. 211).

But something else can be heard in Ahab's utterances, something that is not under the control of his drive to hunt and its murderous articulations. His language, exposed to the wound of the whale's address, collapses into a series of almost inarticulate *cries and shouts*. Caught between the wound to the body and the wound to the soul, no longer body and not yet articulated meaning but their in-between, Ahab's language becomes almost nothing but a wail.

The pathos, grandeur, and terror, the immense complexity and the enigma of the character that is Ahab, involve precisely the tension between his language as embodying the drive to hunt the whale and his language as a shattering and pathos laden cry or wail. And nowhere better can this tension be felt than in the two great scenes around which our analysis will revolve. The first of these is the famous Quarter-deck scene, where Ahab addresses the sailors for the first time and reveals the secret mission which drives him:

> Vehemently pausing he [Ahab] *cried*:—
> "What do you do when you see a whale, men?"
> "Sing out for him!" was the impulsive rejoinder from a score of clubbed voices.
> "Good!" *cried Ahab*, with a wild approval in his tones; observing the hearty *animation* into which his *unexpected question* had so magnetically thrown them. . . .
> More and more strangely and fiercely glad and approving, grew the countenance of the old man at every shout; while the mariners began to gaze curiously at each other, *as if marvelling how it was that they themselves became so excited at such seemingly purposeless questions*. . . .
> "All ye mast-headers have before now heard me give orders about a white whale. Look ye! d'ye see this Spanish ounce of gold?"—*holding up a broad bright coin to the sun*—"it is a sixteen dollar piece, men—a doubloon. . . .
> . . . exhibiting the gold with the other [hand] and with a high raised voice exclaiming: "Whosoever of ye raises me a white-headed whale with a wrinkled brow and a crooked jaw; whosoever of ye raises me that white-headed whale, with three holes punctured in his starboard fluke—look ye, whosoever of ye raises me that same white-headed whale, . . . he shall have this gold ounce, my boys!"
> "Huzza! huzza!" cried the seamen, as with swinging tarpaulins they hailed the act of nailing the gold to the mast. . . .
> "Captain Ahab," said Tashtego, "that white whale must be the same that some call Moby Dick."
> "Moby Dick?" *shouted Ahab*. "Do you know the white whale then, Tash?" . . .

"Captain Ahab, I have heard of Moby Dick—but it was not Moby Dick that took off thy leg?" . . .

"Aye, Starbuck; aye, my hearties all round; it was Moby Dick that dismasted me; Moby Dick that brought me to this dead stump I stand on now. Aye, aye," he *shouted with a terrific, loud, animal sob*, like that of a heart-stricken moose; "Aye, aye! It was that accursed white whale that razeed me; made a poor pegging lubber of me for ever and a day!" Then tossing both arms, with measureless imprecations he *shouted out*: "Aye, aye! and *I'll chase him round Good Hope, and round the Horn, and round the Norway Maelstrom, and round perdition's flames before I give him up*. And this is what ye have shipped for, men! *to chase that white whale on both sides of land, and over all sides of earth, till he spouts black blood and rolls fin out*. What say ye, men, will ye splice hands on it, now? I think ye do look brave."

"*Aye, aye!" shouted the harpooners and seamen* . . .

"'God bless ye," he seemed to *half sob and half shout*. "God bless ye, men." (pp. 161–63)

The wounding whale, experienced at first by Ahab as an enigmatic address, has now become a *wounding wail*, addressed to the sailors and experienced by them as an enigmatic and astonishing question. Before any understanding of Ahab's statement as a meaning, it is the very fact that he addresses them in a cry that constitutes the initial impact and power of his speech. And just as the address of the wounding whale meant a loss of Ahab's mastery over meanings and at the same time was an inspiring call for life, so Ahab's cries and shouts are a perplexing and surprising address that destabilizes the sailors who *do not know as who* or what they are addressed, but simply find *that* they are addressed. The sailors have lost control over themselves and *marvel* at their own actions, which they do not understand, but at the same time they are filled with enthusiasm, are inspired, and respond to the cries as to an animating and revolutionary call for life.

Thus the *linguistic* address, understood now as a cry or a wail, comes to occupy a similar position to the address of the whale for Ahab; that is, the position we have located between the exposure to the bodily wound and the inscription of meaning sensed in this wound. Language, before being the vehicle for stated and stable meanings to be communicated between interlocutors who share an understanding, proves to be an enigmatic, incomprehensible, pathos-laden, and surprising wild cry addressed at sea by an other. Or otherwise put, before it is a comprehensible language whose truth-value can be judged, language as address is marvelous, astonishing, and incredible; in short *language is a fabulous and monstrous wail, which is at the same time a disastrous and wounding wail.*

We can say that what is heard and experienced in this fabulous and disastrous cry is Ahab's wound. The cry thus has the character of a transmission of, and an infliction with, a *singular* bleeding scar, which is at the same time an enigmatic letter. *A scar-letter or a scar(let) letter is the very definition of the cry.*[15] Language testifies first of all to this wound at its heart, which is the cry or the wail, and it is thus first of all an addressed, enigmatic stigma, and perhaps the most adequate verb to describe the act that is the linguistic address is the verb "to wale."[16]

Yet while Ahab by his utterances and cries can indeed be said to transmit the scar, and while the power of his speech is indeed initially the singular power of his shattering cries, the intention of his words and actions is precisely an opposition to, and refusal of, this discovery of the helplessness at the heart of his language. For what Ahab desires so intensely, that toward which he is driven and which possesses his language, is precisely to be freed of this scarlet letter that burns in his flesh, resounds in his cries, and puts him to shame, this mark that is actually the origin and cause of his desire. And it is this desire that becomes the hunt for Moby Dick: "Ah, God! What trances of torments does that man endure who is consumed with one unachieved *revengeful desire*" (p. 201).

Thus desire, this unquenchable striving, originates, as we have seen, in the gap or the distance between the address of the whale/wail and the marked and wounded body. We might say that desire is a directed and oriented response to this surprising enigma that is the address of the whale, it is a dynamic pointer to an address which can neither be recognized nor assimilated into known and familiar categories nor assigned a specific meaning, location, or even existence. Ahab's hunt for the enigmatic and mystic body of the whale, understood now as an adventure of desire, thus seems to bring together two pivotal moments, an erotic moment and a linguistic moment, both of which tend toward violence and terror, for *Ahab's desire is the desire of the tyrant*.[17]

Let us see how all this comes together. We have seen that the wounding address of the whale involves the enigmatic introduction of the dimension of meaning into the vulnerable body, which revealed the relation between the two meanings of "sense." Thus the whale, by marking the exposed and vulnerable sensitive body, can be said to orient and call its sensitive and sensual surfaces, through giving their exposure a certain shape and fixity, and simultaneously to constitute the body as a body subjected to sense and meaning, vulnerable to being called to and oriented.[18] The erotic realm and the openness to signification thus both originate at the limits between the exposed sensitive body and an address to which it is subjected. The wounding whale should therefore be understood to be a seductive agent and, at the same time, an enigma, an incomprehensible meaning.[19]

Both the seduction and the enigma expose the sovereign and proud Ahab to his fundamental helplessness and vulnerability, and it is precisely this exposure, suffered as shame, that he refuses to accept. Thus his desire, which is both a sexual drive and an interpretative one, desires to precisely self destruct, desires to erase itself as a witness to his shame, desires to destroy the wounding and seductive agent that called it into being and has founded it as torment and as jealousy.[20] From the point of view of his adventure as erotic, Dark Ahab, wounded by Eros, therefore wishes to possess the white body of the whale as a beloved's desirable and demonic body (a des-demonic body), which has to be suffocated and destroyed for the shame of desire to be effaced.[21]

From the point of view of his adventure as hermeneutic, Ahab's drive to hunt the whale can be said to be a drive and a desire to destroy the whale/wail at the origin of meaning, to annihilate the wail which testified to meaning's dependence upon the passivity of the body and its necessary relation to an address. It is a drive and a desire to be oneself the origin of meaning, to be able to master one's own passivity and give it meaning.[22] Ahab dreams of a meaning without a body, or of a body, in which the wound is spiritualized and consumed completely into meaning; he dreams of being "the unconquerable captain in the soul" (p. 560).

It is in this way that desire becomes a desire for mastery, and it is thus that the language of desire becomes a language of tyranny and terror: and this in two senses—both in the sense that Ahab's desirous hunt is an attempt of his language to master its own origin, a refusal to accept its passivity, and in the sense that everything and everyone has to be mastered as tools to achieve this single purpose.

Yet this mastery of the others as tools involves more than the practical purpose of hunting the whale. More essentially—and it is here that the political dimension of Ahab's drive and desire has to be thought—it is concerned with a necessity of his language's desire to *reduce into one* all other languages and voices. If the ship, with the plurality of races and tongues of its crew,—and of course as an allegory of this new, yet unapproachable America—can be described as a miraculous post-Babel achievement, then the desire of Ahab's language to master itself and master meaning cannot be achieved unless the world before Babel is restored, where there is only one tongue and language, therefore, can perfectly correspond to itself and declare itself the absolute master.[23]

The hunt thus reduces into oneness the multiplicity and plurality of life on the *Pequod*: "The wind that made great bellies of their sails, and rushed the vessel on by arms invisible as irresistible; this seemed the symbol of *that unseen agency which so enslaved them to the race. They were one man, not thirty*. For as the one ship that held them all; though it was put together of all contrasting things—oak, and maple, and pine wood; iron, and pitch, and hemp—yet all these ran into each other in the one concrete hull, which shot on its way, both balanced and directed by the long, central keel; even so all the individualities of the crew, this man's valor, that man's fear; guilt and guiltlessness, all varieties were *welded into oneness, and were all directed to that fatal goal which Ahab their one lord and keel did point to*"[24] (p. 557).

What enabled Ahab's extraordinary feat of controlling and uniting the sailors is first and foremost the addressed and wounding wail, which has shattered their identity, has contagiously infected them, and has exposed them to the enigma of their vulnerability. The addressed cry in this way seems to open up the possibility of complete mastery and unification of the sailors precisely because of the almost complete destruction of identity that it entails. The sailors, I have mentioned earlier, in the moment of their surprise, do not know who they are, and it is precisely in this moment that the possibility opens for Ahab to assign them an identity, to name them anew, and to call them to a new destiny. This seems to be accomplished through the raising of the fetishized gold coin, which fixes their confusion and directs the enthusiasm of their lives to Ahab's destructive purpose.[25] Ahab's wail thus seems to have transformed the sailors into a drive, Ahab's drive, and has united them all in their quest for a common object of desire.

Thus to sum up this discussion of the Quarter-deck scene, the tension that resonates in Ahab's address to the sailors involves, from Ahab's point of view, the relation between his wounded language as a terrible cry and a loss of stable language, and his wounded language as a driven tyrannical language trying to overcome the discovery of its own passivity. From the point of view of the sailors who are addressed, the tension structuring their adventure is one that exists between their event of being wounded by the wail, which is both an inspiring call for life and a loss of identity and authority over themselves, and the domination by Ahab's drive which has managed to infiltrate their wound and give it shape and direction.

Yet I have said that this tension structuring Ahab is manifested in an exemplary way in another great passage, an extraordinarily powerful dream scene:

> Often, when forced from his hammock by exhausting and intolerably vivid dreams of the night, which, resuming his own intense thoughts through the day, carried them on amid a clashing of phrensies, and whirled them round and round in his blazing brain, till the very throbbing of his *life-spot* became insufferable anguish; and when, as was sometimes the case, these spiritual throes

Ahab's Whale

in him heaved his being up from its base, and a chasm seemed opening in him, from which forked flames and lightnings shot up, and accursed fiends beckoned him to leap down among them; when this hell in himself yawned beneath him, *a wild cry* would be heard through the ship; and with glaring eyes Ahab would burst from his state room, as though escaping from a bed that was on fire. *Yet these, perhaps, instead of being the unsuppressable symptoms of some latent weakness, or fright at his own resolve, were but the plainest tokens of its intensity.* For, at such times, crazy Ahab, the scheming *unappeasedly steadfast hunter of the white whale*; this Ahab that had gone to his hammock was not the agent that so caused him to burst from it in horror again.

The latter was the eternal, *living principle* or soul in him; and in sleep, being for the time dissociated from the characterizing mind, which at other times employed it for its outer vehicle or agent, it spontaneously sought escape from the scorching contiguity of the frantic thing, of which, for the time, it was no longer an integral. But as the mind does not exist unless leagued with the soul, therefore it must have been that, in Ahab's case, yielding up all his thought and fancies to his one supreme purpose; that purpose, by its own sheer inveteracy of will, forced itself against gods and devils into a kind of self-assumed, independent being of its own. Nay, could grimly live and burn, while the *common vitality* to which it was conjoined, fled horror-stricken from the unbidden and unfathered birth. Therefore, the tormented spirit that glared out of bodily eyes, when what seemed Ahab rushed from his room, was for a time but a vacated thing, a formless somnambulistic being, *a ray of living light*, to be sure, but without an object to color, and therefore a *blankness in itself.* (pp. 201–2)

Ahab's dream complicates further the enigmatic manifestations of the address of the whale. Let us briefly follow this complication and implication of Ahab and the whale and the terms and structures it brings into play.

"It is because 'real life,'" writes Shoshana Felman, "is nothing other than a gaping hole that Dream, little by little, pours into it. Loss becomes a doorway opening onto the 'invisible world.'"[26] The dismemberment and terrible open wound caused by the address of the whale has now become, precisely, the doorway opening onto the invisible world. But, as Ishmael says, "in many of its aspects this visible world seems formed in love, the invisible spheres were formed in fright."[27] The question of the dream, and of the horror and anxiety it involves, is introduced into Ahab's adventure as marking how the address of the whale, by remaining an unknowable, inassimilable, and unmasterable event which cannot be understood as unified meaning, keeps infinitely[28] repeating in dreams as the attempt of the wounded subject to restore its mastery and to regain knowledge, that is, to heal the wound at its heart.

A dream, the novel seems to suggest, is perhaps, metaphorically, always the dream of the addressed and wounded captain trying to regain his/her stability and mastery of meaning. The dream is thus, perhaps always, the dream of the "unappeasedly steadfast hunter of the white whale."[29] What distinguishes Ahab's dream is its *literalness*; in it the cause of the dream, i.e. the address of the whale, corresponds to the dream's content as the fulfillment of the desire of the tyrant, i.e. the wounding by and the successful hunt of the whale.[30] Ahab's dream thus testifies to the birth of dream in the wound—it is a dream that literally shows its own birth and its own cause.

But while the address of the whale seems to have as its response a tyrannical dream that testifies to a desire to hunt, something else can be heard from within Ahab's dream, something that is not under the control of this desire and its murderous dreams, and this is, precisely, a wild cry, a wild, white (or *blank*) wail. Indeed, the whale that addressed Ahab from "without" and has shattered his stability and his wholeness has now turned into a wild wail that cries out and haunts Ahab from "within" and interrupts the dream of wholeness regained.[31] This cry, this wail, is the *cry of life* that *resists* being turned into a dream. That is, it is the *shocking discovery of life* itself (and of the whale as the address of life) as a principle of resistance to the desire of the tyrant or the hunter, the desire to erase the address of the whale.[32]

It is as if the wound itself, this exposure of the helpless living body to the mark of the address of the whale/wail, cries out refusing to be healed, cries out as an awakening, resistant, and insistent witness to the injustice done to the living in the name of the burning dream. It is this wild white cry of life, around which I would argue the book as a whole revolves and which it allows to resonate, which tries to free life, and keeps the memory of the address of the whale/wail living; and it might also be understood as the origin of the ethical "thou shall not kill," that is, as a general interdiction on the killing of the living.[33]

Thus summarizing the various movements of the whale as they are manifested in Ahab's adventure, we can say that the whale is all at once: that which one encounters at sea, which wounds and interrupts the stability of the land; that which one desires to destroy and stifle to regain this stability; that which causes the dream of erasing the wound; that which is (in certain kinds of dreams) repeated over and over; and that which, in the dream, resists being turned into a dream, the awakening cry of life.[34] Ahab's cry (for the cry is always singular), is Moby Dick, or the white whale; or we might say, Moby Dick or the white wail.[35]

This principle of resistance that is life involves as well the introduction of the vocabulary of power, this time as intensity. In this case as well, it is the discovery of the enigmatic relations and interdependence between life, the wound, and the whale that calls for a vocabulary of power. It is precisely the collapse of the false stability of the dream and the chasm and abyss of horror discovered at its heart, the chasm that is precisely the revelation of the relation between the exposed wound and the whale/wail which shatters the subject from "within" and shows it to be dependent on an "external" address, which brings to light these enigmatic relations.

Thus we can see/hear/taste/smell/touch/feel . . . again how whale-thinking, that is, the thinking that takes the address of the whale and its implications into account, always demands the introduction of the vocabulary of power.

It is as if the address of the whale/wail, this enigmatic, maddening, diabolical, horrifying, seductive, and revolutionary disorientation of the senses, which reminds us of and calls for a certain rediscovery or perhaps reinvention of language as cry, of the body as wound, of life as mourning and as enthusiasm, and of the senses (in all their various meanings) as vulnerable exposure and event, also reminds us of a certain inevitable vocabulary that has to be thought and rethought, rediscovered and invented, the vocabulary of power and of forces.

It will be the tasks of the following discussions to illuminate a bit further the necessity and implications of this vocabulary.

4
Ishmael's Whale—Whiteness and the Witness, or the Collapse of the Author

> Death: not, first of all, annihilation, non-being, or nothingness, but a certain experience for the survivor of the "without-response" . . . it is the murderer who would like to identify death with nothingness
> —Jacques Derrida, from words delivered upon the death of Emmanuel Levinas

How does the question of the address of the whale/wail, which has guided our reading of the book, open up in relation to Ishmael?

Ishmael, we have seen, can be said to occupy mainly three positions: 1) He is a character participating, more or less, in the action of the narrated events which constitute the main story-line of the novel. 2) He is a whale-author, a writer whose work is dedicated to the enigma of the whale. 3) He is an ambiguous narrator the status of whose speech trembles between that of fabulist telling stories of monsters and adventures at sea and a witness to unspeakable, monstrous, horrors and an overwhelming loss of life.

It is the task of any attempt to understand the full implications of the address of the whale/wail in Ishmael's case to think the logic that unites the various relations to the whale as they are manifested in these three positions. It is to this task that we now turn.

THE POWER OF WHITENESS

"What the white whale was to Ahab, has been hinted; what, at times, he was to me, as yet remains unsaid. Aside from those more obvious considerations touching Moby Dick, which could not but occasionally awaken in any man's soul some alarm, there was another thought, or rather vague, nameless horror concerning him, which at times by its intensity completely overpowered all the rest; and yet so mystical and well nigh ineffable was it, that I almost despair of putting it in a comprehensible form. It was the whiteness of the whale that above all things appalled me. But how can I hope to explain myself here; and yet, in some dim, random way, explain myself I must, else all these chapters might be naught" (p. 188).

Thus opens what is perhaps the most famous and enigmatic chapter in the novel, "The Whiteness of the Whale." If in Ahab's case Moby Dick was addressed as a bodily wound, then in Ishmael's case he is addressed as horrifying and appalling[1] whiteness. Understanding, in Ishmael's case, what the address of the whale involves, forces us, then, to think what the exposure to whiteness means. I therefore argue that it is precisely through an investigation of the singular nature of this enigmatic exposure to whiteness, or to the white whale/wail, that the relations among the various rhetorical positions from which Ishmael speaks can be elucidated. That is, the relations among a character experiencing overwhelming events, an analytic writer trying to account for and exhaust a certain enigma, and a fabulist/witness telling a marvelous story/testifying to an unspeakable disaster.[2]

Ishmael himself conducts this investigation into whiteness in this chapter, presenting himself as an analytic thinker and as an investigator into an overwhelming enigma: "But not yet have we *solved* the incantation of this whiteness, and learned why it *appeals with such power* to the soul" (p. 195).

Let us, then, follow at least partly the extraordinarily complex investigation into whiteness conducted here. What is made plain by the quotation cited above is that the exposure to whiteness is an overwhelming and enigmatic event that calls for the vocabulary of power. This recalls the way the vocabulary of power is introduced in the case of Ahab's wound to mark the event of the collapse of the commander's ability to give sense and orientation, to master language. In Ishmael's case as well, the introduction of this vocabulary in relation to the experience of whiteness marks the collapse of his *ability* to speak and make sense, to be the master and author of a coherent story concerning that which happened to him; Ishmael no longer knows who he is or what this whiteness wants of him. But whiteness is also the place in which the imperative to tell his story originates. What is it in whiteness that brings about this collapse, asks the surprised and horrified Ishmael, what is the meaning of whiteness?

Ishmael begins his investigation by attempting, precisely, to assign whiteness a specific meaning, to isolate a certain fixed, symbolic value that can be attached to it. In what is by far the longest sentence in the book, Ishmael breathlessly looks for and fails to find a meaningful place to rest, such respite continually postponed by his uneasy feeling that in every suggestion he makes there still is something missing which, if found, would finally account for the full significance of whiteness and leave him satisfied and in peace.

Let us take a look at this long sentence as representative of the rhetorical strategy of this chapter in particular and of Ishmael's discourse in general: "*Though* in many natural objects, whiteness refiningly enhances beauty, as if imparting some special virtue of its own, as in marbles, japonicas, and pearls; and *though* various nations have in some way recognised a certain *royal* pre-eminence in this hue; even the barbaric, *grand old kings* of Pegu placing the title 'Lord of the White Elephants' above all their other magniloquent ascriptions of *dominion*; and the modern kings of Siam unfurling the same snow-white quadruped in the royal standard; and the Hanoverian flag bearing the one figure of a snow-white charger; and the great Austrian *Empire*, Caesarian heir to overlording Rome, having for the imperial color the same imperial hue; and though this pre-eminence in it applies to the human race itself, giving the *white man ideal mastership* over every dusky tribe; and *though*, besides all this, whiteness has been even made significant of gladness, for among the Romans a white stone marked a joyful day; and though in other mortal sympathies and symbolizings, this same hue is made the emblem of many touching, noble things—the innocence of brides, the benignity of age; though among the Red Men of America the giving of the white belt of wampum was the deepest pledge of honor; though in many climes, whiteness typifies the majesty of Justice in the ermine of the J*udge,* and contributes to the daily state of kings and queens drawn by milk-white steeds; though even in the higher mysteries of the most august religions it has been made the symbol of the *divine spotlessness and power*; by the Persian fire worshippers, the white forked flame being held the holiest on the altar; and in the Greek mythologies, Great Jove himself being made incarnate in a snow-white bull; and though to the noble Iroquois, the midwinter sacrifice of the sacred White Dog was by far the holiest festival of their theology, that spotless, faithful, creature being held the purest envoy they could send to the Great Spirit with the annual tidings of their own fidelity; and though directly from the Latin word for white, all Christian *priests* derive the name of one part of their sacred vesture, the alb or tunic, worn beneath the cassock; though in the Vision of St. John, white robes are given to the redeemed, and the four-and-twenty elders stand clothed in white before the great white throne, and the Holy One that sitteth there white like wool; *yet* for all these accumulated associations, with whatever is sweet, and honorable, and sublime, there yet lurks an elusive something in the innermost idea of this hue, which *strikes more of panic to the soul* than that redness which affrights in *blood*" (pp. 188–89).

This extraordinary, bleeding sentence is helpless Ishmael's way of responding to the shock that was the encounter with whiteness, or with the white whale. Its rhythm of dissatisfaction, which takes the form of the stuttering "though . . . though . . . yet" and which quite obviously can be continued infinitely, shows the encounter with, or the exposure to, whiteness as an event in which the quest for meaning opens as, precisely, a "*not yet* have we *solved* the incantation of this whiteness" (p. 195). Thus we can say that before any specific and well-understood *this* or *that* stable meaning, there is an addressed and overwhelming white riddle that opens the quest for meaning as an attempt at response. We can also see that this quest for meaning is the opening of temporality as the relation between an overwhelming and unassimilable white event which has happened and which opens the past and memory, and a search for the meaning of this event which extends and opens the future as that which has always not yet arrived.

Let us examine in greater detail the way in which this strange whiteness opens Ishmael's discourse and operates in it. Two things seem to be quite evident from a first look at the list of qualities that Ishmael brings to try to solve the riddle of whiteness and assign it a specific meaning: 1) This list is potentially infinite, it can never really be closed—there can be as many examples to the value of whiteness as there are values and meanings in general. No one and final meaning can be found to account for whiteness. And 2) taking this first point to its inevitable conclusion we can say that whiteness can be associated with *any* meaning or value whatsoever, and it is precisely this characteristic, this emptiness (or fullness), that, finally, reveals it as horrifying.[3] This seems to suggest that whiteness is a double principle: a) It is the principle of the *possibility or potentiality of inscription* of any meaning whatsoever, and thus the *horrifying discovery of whiteness* is a discovery of a white surface or page which *can* be stained, or wounded. b) It is a restless, *dynamic* principle, operating invisibly and inaudibly behind every meaning, preventing it from ever closing in upon itself and instituting itself as final and as master of all other meanings, always calling it to move on.

This dual formulation of the principle of whiteness has to be articulated together with another, paradoxical formulation of Ishmael's that occurs toward the end of the chapter: "is it, that as in essence whiteness is not so much a color as the visible absence of color, and at the same time the concrete of all colors . . . there is such a *dumb blankness, full of meaning*, in a wide landscape of snows—a colorless, all-color of atheism from which we shrink?" (p. 195). This seems to suggest that the encounter with the riddle or enigma of whiteness is an event that overflows with an overwhelming excess, or even explosion, of meaning, and at the same time lacks meaning altogether, represents the exhaustion and limit of any possibility of meaning. Or, put a bit differently, it is an event that marks the overwhelming birth of meaning and, at the same time, its complete disaster.

Yet these characteristics of whiteness would still remain empty and abstract unless we take into account that whiteness for Ishmael is not presented as simply marking an impersonal enigma which he attempts to analyze, but rather it *marks him as a white, and monstrous, riddle to himself* and has to do with *who*[4] he is. The analysis of whiteness is essentially an investigation in which the "subject" of analysis, the one who analyzes, is implicated, and comes into question. Whiteness, or the white whale/wail, is always whiteness *for or to someone*, and it thus has to do essentially with the one who encounters it; it therefore necessarily raises the question of address. "What the white whale was *to Ahab* has been hinted; what, at times, he was *to me*, as yet remains unsaid" (p. 188). In encountering whiteness Ishmael, destabilized and perplexed, knows *that* he is addressed, but not *as who*[5] he is addressed, and his white discourse is therefore simultaneously an attempt to answer the enigma of who he is as well as an investigation into the riddle of whiteness in general.

But we can say even more about Ishmael's involvement with the riddle of whiteness: "But thou sayest, methinks this white-lead chapter about whiteness is but a white flag hung out from a craven soul; thou surrenderest to a hypo, Ishmael" (p. 194). At the center of this white chapter Ishmael quite suddenly calls himself by name into the seemingly objective and scientific investigation, as if *called upon as an accused* to justify and give testimony, or at least to persuade his readers of the veracity of his extraordinary claims, which seem to exceed any known standards of scientific investigation or juridical proof and to hint at some purely psychological morbidity. Besides giving more and more examples, there is no way for Ishmael to *prove the existence* of this horrible and demonic power of which he speaks, and finally he can only affirm its existence without proof, that is, admitting to the inadequacy of the vocabulary of knowledge: "Though *neither knows* where lie the nameless things of which the mystic sign gives forth such hints; yet with me . . . somewhere those things must exist" (pp. 194–95).

Thus we might say that the perplexed Ishmael, riddle-stricken and tormented, has lost in his encounter with whiteness his stable identity, his *ability to say* who he is, and to knowingly account for and explain what has happened to him, and that he finds himself destitute and accused.[6] He can say almost nothing about who he is, since *who he is can be said to be, precisely, the one addressed by a white riddle.* What he finds in himself when exposed to this white horror, what he finds in place of a secure and stable self, is the enigma of "a formless, somnambulistic being, a ray of living light, to be sure, but without an object to color, and therefore a blankness in itself."[7]

Already discernible from our findings so far is whiteness as a principle of the breakdown of mastery over meanings in general and the collapse of the self's mastery over its own meaning, over who he/she is. From this perspective, we can see that Ishmael's examples in the long passage cited above, though they cannot be granted any essential privilege in getting closer to the meaning of whiteness, are nevertheless not arbitrary. Ishmael seems to privilege examples that mostly pertain to various kinds of institutional power and mastery, such as the symbols of empires, kings, priests, and judges, or those suggesting the mastery of the white race. All these institutions try, precisely, to fix the horrifying and destabilizing principle of whiteness into a single value or meaning which they could dominate and which will symbolize their domination (and in the case of the white race it is quite obvious that it is not white at all and that whiteness is thus used as a metaphorical attempt of this race to master the meaning of that which undermines every stable meaning and identity). Yet it is precisely whiteness that prevents their domination from ever being complete and is in a way the principle of their collapse. This is evidenced (although it is not something which Ishmael himself articulates) by the way that no meaning which an empire, a judge, or a priest assigned to whiteness can ever stop Ishmael's discourse, which is to say dominate it; these authorities and institutions are all erased and washed away by the huge white wave that carries Ishmael's language. But it is not only these empires and institutions that are toppled; Ishmael's attempts to institute himself as master of whiteness and as the solver of its enigma are also brought low.

This is why, finally, Ishmael sees whiteness as essentially more a principle of horror and of the demonic than of goodness. While goodness seeks to establish the highest value from which all other values derive, horror and the demonic are precisely the principles of destruction that annihilate all values and identities, be they good or bad. Whiteness is a riddle beyond good and bad.[8]

Yet we can also discern in these discussions another inevitable level of ambiguity permeating the white Ishmaelian discourse. On the one hand, this will be a courageously proliferating discourse, refusing to stop and be satisfied with any one meaning for the enigma which haunts him (in this case whiteness and, later on, the enigma of the whale in general, about whom the discourse is governed by the same rhetorical strategy); a *moving* discourse (in both senses of the term) which sustains the call of whiteness alive against any attempts at domination.

On the other hand, it is precisely a discourse which, like Ahab's hunt of all the other whales but Moby Dick, refuses to stop and be satisfied by any temporary meaning, and seems overcome by some insatiable drive and a desire for a final meaning and a forever unreachable place of rest. A discourse seeming to proliferate infinitely and without exhaustion, as if to cover up the white surface upon which it is written and to erase all trace of the horror which has set its language going, and thus finally to institute itself as master over whiteness; a discourse that treats the riddle of whiteness as that which can be *solved* and eliminated as a consequence. Thus if I have said earlier that Ahab's language involves a tension between a language of a drive to hunt the whale and a shattering and pathetic cry or wail, it seems that we may now say that Ishmael's language involves the tension between a drive to write over the whiteness of the whale and a moving act of witnessing to the inaudible and enigmatic language of the white whale/wail.[9]

Or perhaps we should say, even more accurately, and in relation to the formulation of Ahab's wounded languages we attempted to articulate, that in Ishmael's case as well we should distinguish between his restless language, which is possessed by a drive to write over whiteness and reach a final meaning, and something else, another language which *speaks through* Ishmael's writing (for Ishmael himself never formulates the functioning of whiteness as we do); and this is the moving language of witnessing the white whale/wail.

Therefore, the writing of whiteness seems to involve an essential ambiguity that perhaps cannot be overcome. Its central problem is how a language can testify to the enigma of whiteness without actually becoming a language of mastery that covers over whiteness in the very attempt to witness it. Or, viewed from a slightly different yet highly related perspective, and put into Ahabian terminology, how can one respond to the encounter with the white whale in such a way that would not be a murderous hunt, but that would keep the whale/wail alive? Is there such a language, is there such a non-murderous response? This, I argue, is one of the major questions involved in the event of language this novel tries to bring about. It will be a task of our following discussions to try to testify to such an attempt.

I have begun to suggest that Ishmael's encounter with whiteness has an essential relation to his encounter with Ahab. Understanding what the riddle of whiteness means in Ishmael's case cannot be separated from understanding the enigma that Ahab is *for* Ishmael: "So *powerfully* did the whole grim aspect of Ahab *affect me*, and the *livid brand* which streaked it, that for the first few moments I hardly noted that not a little of this overbearing grimness was owing to the barbaric *white leg* on which he partly stood" (p. 124). Ishmael's powerful encounter with Ahab is thus described as an encounter with an addressing white scar, with a branded mark, or with an enigmatic, white stigma. Indeed, a paragraph earlier, Ishmael describes Ahab's scar as "a slender rod-like mark, lividly whitish . . . whether that mark was born with him, or whether it was the scar left by some desperate wound, no one could certainly say" (p. 123). Therefore, based on our previous discussions, we can say that Ahab addresses Ishmael as a white cry, or as a white wail.

This seems to suggest that Ishmael's encounter with whiteness has to be thought of as a wounding encounter, but it also calls for a new understanding of the wound as, precisely, an addressed whiteness. The wound, the cry, and whiteness have to be thought together. Ishmael's unique white adventure seems to involve precisely the discovery of the relations among these three terms. And it is precisely this discovery that differentiates Ishmael's exposure to Ahab's cries, and it is this discovery that lies at the heart of his becoming a witness/fabulist. Let us see how.

I have argued that Ahab addressed the entire body of sailors as a wounding cry or as a wail; yet in Ishmael's case something separates him from the sailors. Describing his reactions to Ahab's enflaming cries Ishmael recalls that he, at first, participated in the common fascination: "I, Ishmael, was one of that crew; *my shouts* had gone up with the rest; my oath had been welded with theirs; and *stronger I shouted,* and *more did I hammer* and clinch my oath, because of the dread in my soul. A wild, mystical, *sympathetical feeling* was in me; Ahab's quenchless feud seemed mine. With greedy ears I learned the history of that murderous monster against whom I and all the others had taken our oaths of violence and revenge" (p. 179).

Ahab's cries and shouts became Ishmael's cries and shouts, his pathos elicited a sympathetic response, and his violence became also Ishmael's violence. Yet a certain dread and horror seem to separate Ishmael from the rest of the sailors, and to make his cries and shouts somehow different. Toward the end of the chapter this difference is articulated as an enigmatic question raised by Ishmael, a question that already separates him from the rest of the crew: "How it was that *they* so aboundingly responded to the old man's ire—by what evil magic *their souls were possessed,* that at times his hate *seemed almost theirs*; the White Whale as much their insufferable foe as his; how all this came to be.... *all this to explain, would be to dive deeper than Ishmael can go*" (p. 187).

Unlike the other sailors, Ishmael, while participating in the hunt, does not close the enigma that was Ahab's cry, is not completely possessed by his drive. The cry and its possessive consequences become an enigma that marks the collapse of Ishmael's capacity for explanation, yet this is a collapse that somehow leaves Ishmael somewhat free of Ahab's drive.

It is on this helpless note and with this enigmatic question that the chapter "Moby Dick" ends, the chapter that described Ahab's hatred of the whale, and the sailors and Ishmael's possession by this driving hate. The following chapter is, precisely, "The Whiteness of the Whale," which opens with the following demarcation and a marking of difference: "What the white whale *was to Ahab*, has been hinted; what, at times, he *was to me*, as yet remains unsaid" (p. 188). Thus Ishmael's question quoted above, with which the chapter "Moby Dick" ends, marks as well the limit between the two chapters and thus the limit between what the whale is for Ahab (Moby Dick) and what it is for Ishmael (White).

Ahab's whale is, finally, not Ishmael's, Ishmael is not completely possessed by Ahab's whale/wail, and *that which separates them, that which marks their difference, is, precisely, the whiteness of the whale/wail*, which is also the whiteness of the page separating the two chapters (41 and 42) as well as the name of the new chapter in which Ishmael's destiny seems to be separated from Ahab's possessive designs. Thus whiteness is revealed to be also a *praxis* of marking a difference, an activity of differentiation in relation to another's possessive whale/wail.

But what does it mean to be separated by whiteness? How can this empty, contentless, and even invisible thing mark the very separation from another's driving possession and desire and be the very *cause of freedom*?[10] That is, it seems we can say that Ishmael's whale is *exactly* Ahab's whale, there is no content, no specific quality or mark of identity, that can distinguish between them, yet they are completely different, with a difference and a differentiation that is white. How can this be?

What these questions seem to suggest is that this whiteness that separates Ishmael from Ahab and the crew, this whiteness that is the cause of his freedom, is *nothing else but Ahab's whale/wail viewed and sustained as an enigmatic address, an enigma which, precisely, singularizes Ishmael*, and has to do with who he is. We can perhaps define now "who" Ishmael the witness is. He is the nameless one, for whom the others' whales, their cries and shouts, their wounds and scars, become an addressing and wounding white enigma, to which he testifies and which mark the very question of his destiny, of his survival, and of his freedom.

Yet freedom is always difficult freedom, for the very white separation from Ahab becomes, in its turn, and as we have already started to see, the cause of a new drive and a new desire to cover the white enigma that was opened. The very wounding cause of freedom turns into a new cause of a drive and of desire. Is there a way to leave whiteness in its enigma?

Let us now try to bring together the various aspects of whiteness that we have raised.

Whiteness is first of all a dynamic principle that exceeds any stabilized meaning or entity. This dynamic principle can only be discovered through an overwhelming and enigmatic event of encounter that revolutionizes the one confronted by this enigma. Being an enigma means, among other things, that this event structurally involves a process of investigation and questioning, yet the one who attempts such an investigation discovers that the first thing the event revolutionized was nothing less than the very ways or forms of asking questions and the well-known demarcations which regular investigations presupposed between an investigator and that which is investigated, between that which is asked about and the one who asks the questions.

When discovering whiteness we discover that we are *no longer able* to raise questions such as "what is whiteness?" or "what is the meaning of whiteness?" but rather we can only ask, and even must ask, the following questions: "*What happened to me* that whiteness all of a sudden *imposed itself* on me, *what power* overwhelmed me, *who* am I, since I don't know any more, why was I so *moved* by this astonishing, monstrous, and unbelievable encounter through which whiteness all of a sudden blinded me, what *should* I do, but also what *forces* me to ask these questions which do not seem to have originated from me, what empty, invisible, white foreign element questions *in* me and questions me as foreign to myself?" But one is also compelled to ask, "did something happen at all, can I be sure that anything occurred, can I trace the place where it originated?" That is, whiteness presents itself as a possible address. *And this, I suggest, is what being addressed means for the novel, it means having something happen to me, to a "me," in which the enigma of who I am is at stake.*[11] This address collapses any illusory conception of the self as a stable identity and reveals the "subject" as empty, helpless, nameless, and abandoned and as originating precisely through this astonishing event of address to which the only possible response is "Who, me?"[12] The effect of this address upon the "me" is such that I can no longer know whether it is me who is asking about whiteness or whether it is whiteness asking about itself through me. But this place where knowledge collapses involves as well a need to communicate, to transmit to others this revolutionary event and tell my story.

Thus the encounter through which whiteness overwhelms constitutes one at one and the same time as: 1) someone burdened with the task of responding to who he/she is; 2) an investigator into this monstrous and enigmatic principle of excess and of the event, or as the locus of this principle's questioning of itself or even revealing itself to itself through me and my investigation;[13] 3) as a witness—in the sense, initially, of the one who reports on that which has happened and was not available to everyone, since obviously a witness is called for only in the case of a certain gap in knowledge. In the case of the enigmatic white event I am necessarily and essentially constituted as a *sole* witness[14] to an event, since the white event is, by definition, that which happened to me and only to me, since it can only be discovered through the structure of something happening to a "me," which has to do with who I am in my singularity. It is the very secret through which I am singularized.[15] To really testify to something, to an event as white, means having been revolutionized by it and having sustained it as an enigma in which who I am is at stake. Thus it is my very being and life, my being alive, that become a testimony to that which happened to me. Everything I say or do becomes an act of witnessing, even if I do not at all recount thematically the events that enigmatically addressed me, and even if I do not know at all what happened.

4) A storyteller/performer who has to communicate and transmit this event that cannot be known, and can do it only by becoming this white event, the way that an actor or performer becomes indistinguishable from a role which has to be performed.[16]

But it is precisely because of the implications of the abovementioned characteristics of whiteness that the very question of a white testimony is put under an essential and constitutive suspicion of, or even an accusation of, fabulation and deception. First, because by definition a white event is that which happens only to me as a sole witness, there can be no external guarantee, no affirming *authority*, that what I say has actually happened, that it is not pure fabrication.[17] Second, because it is not even clear to me, in the case of a white event, that something in fact happened. This is so because the white event means the very collapse of knowledge, since it constituted me as a "me" before I came into being, it called me to myself and chose me before I was there. Whiteness therefore happens in a zone that is prior to this or that stable identity, prior to a possibility of decision of truth or falsity in relation to it.[18] Therefore, we can say that any act of white witnessing carries with it as its shadow the realm of the fabulous—and vice versa.[19] *The white encounter essentially constitutes the "me" as a witness/fabulist, and it marks the very opening of the trembling realm of fictionality*, which is *not* a realm of invented events, but the shadowy and undecidable realm of the trembling between the testimonial and the fabulous.[20]

This powerful, horrifying, surprising and destabilizing encounter through which whiteness overwhelms is, we have seen, a revolutionary event that shatters the "I"'s existence as a subject of knowledge, and as master of himself and of meanings, revealing an empty, helpless, and destitute "who, me?" constituted by and chosen despite itself, waled into being, by a certain excess that is experienced as an address or a call.[21] This event is a horrible disaster and destruction of the self and, at the same time, the very event of its birth. It is thus also, at the same time, the white opening, even the explosion, of all meaning, of the possibility or potentiality for meaning before this or that meaning, and the emptying out, the white erasure, of any previous possibility for meaning, since this event means that everything has changed.

Whiteness as metaphor, and perhaps as something more than metaphor, thus marks at the same time 1) the self as an empty, contentless potentiality for meaning and inscription rather than a stable this or that meaning. 2) The self as burdened with the task and the imperative of responding to who he/she is, yet lacking content or prescription for the fulfillment of this task; thus, the self as burdened with a white imperative, with a white call that does not tell it what to do, but only that it is called and has to respond.[22] 3) The event itself, because of its nature of surprise and unknowability, as colorless and invisible—whiteness as that which exceeds any possibility of knowledge and perception, since it is what opens them and makes them possible, and thus evades them and seems white. 4) The verbal occurrence, the whitening, as the opening and birth of all meaning and the destruction of every meaning.

But I have also said that whiteness has to be essentially thought of in relation to the cry and to the wound. The encounter with whiteness is an encounter with a wounding cry. How do these come together? Let us start with the cry.

We have seen that being exposed to language as a cry meant experiencing a shattering address, whose content is unknown, through which I know *that* I am addressed and chosen by language (i.e. that there is signification), that the enigma of who I am is at stake; yet what this cry that is a white letter in a bottle wants from me is unknown. The cry is thus an enigmatic and incomprehensible event of speech in which the stable language of the self is destroyed and a white call is heard. What is heard in this cry whose white incomprehensibility constitutes me as a "who, me?" is, at the same time, the white opening of speech, or the birth and fullness of every possibility for meaning—that is, the excess of language over specific words saying this or that; the white exhaustion and collapse of speech into inarticulateness and loss, the emptiness of all meanings; and my very self, the enigma or riddle that I am, as a trembling white cry or wail that both bears witness, as a white echoing, to the cry that addressed it, and has the triple task of responding to who he/she is, investigating the enigma of the cry, and reverberating or performing this cry, that opened in an immemorial past (that is, a past not available to me as memory, since it called me and chose me, waled me before I came into being) to the future and for the sake of the future.

The term that strikes me as bringing together most successfully all these characteristics of the cry is the term pathos. *The event of the cry is an event of pathos*, the thought of the cry is the thought of pathos. Pathos as I understand it is no longer to be grasped as the expression of a subjective emotion, but rather it is to be thought of in relation to its Greek origin as "to suffer that which happens," a white event of a cry that shatters the subject and chooses a "me" to respond to it, and in which who I am is at stake.

Yet I have also argued that what is heard and transmitted in this cry of pathos is the wound. Being exposed to Ahab's cry also means being inflicted with his wound. Yet this wound, as we have seen, is of a special kind, it is not a simple bodily wound, but it is a wound experienced as an address—no longer simply body and not yet stable spiritual meaning but their in-between. I have attempted to define this entanglement of the wound and the address that is transmitted in the cry as a relation between a scar and a letter, a scar(let)-letter, in which can be read, heard, or seen, touched, and felt. . . . the enigmatic relations that constitute the human body between exposed surfaces of sensitivity capable of being wounded and a subjection to meaning and orientation.

If we now reformulate the white address or the call as a

wounding of this special kind, in which the enigma of who I am is at stake, we might say that the call, this seductive and enigmatic address, is the immemorial event in which the human shamefully discovers its helpless nudity and absolute vulnerability, its exposure to other bodies apprehended as forces,[23] that is, in which the human living body discovers itself as a *capacity* for being wounded and therefore as a capacity for being oriented, i.e. a capacity to know good from bad, before this or that meaning and orientation.

This wounding call through which the "me" discovers, ashamed, its living nudity is at the same time a singularizing call and that which dispossesses me, and being exposed to it means that I both have to respond to it, call it by name, and be responsible to it, although I do not know what it wants from me. I also have the task of responding to who I am in front of it, that is, to justify my existence, my life, which is exposed to its judgment.

We have therefore seen how whiteness, the cry, and the wound belong together, and I would suggest that the very term that unites them for the novel and demands their being thought together is Life.

Two Understandings of the Fabulous

Before turning to examine Ishmael's status as a whale-author let us briefly try to expand a little on the notion of the fabulous. We are now in a better position to understand the fabulous, and it is necessary for us to grasp its full implications in order to see how it functions in Ishmael's discourse.

If earlier we have associated the fabulous mainly with the constitutive possibility of deceit inherent in the logic of the white event, we should perhaps now expand the description of the fabulous and show how it is essentially related to the white event in another manner as well, for only all these meanings of the fabulous brought together could explain the complexity and the necessity of bringing it to bear as a key term in a reading of *Moby-Dick* which I see as a *fabulous novel of testimony*.

The *Oxford English Dictionary* indicates that the fabulous has to do with mainly three meanings—1) something astonishing and incredible; 2) something fictional; 3) something mythical, legendary, and ahistorical. It seems to me that there are mainly two ways to understand the relations among these three meanings and thus two ways to understand the fabulous. The first one, inadequate (as this book attempts to show) but nonetheless prevalent in many traditional conceptions of literature, would be to understand it as denoting the imaginative invention of fictive worlds, of non-existent, strange, and monstrous beings that we do not usually encounter and which thus astonish us and strike our curiosity simply by their unfamiliarity. We *know* that these inventions are inventions, that they cannot be assigned a reality, and cannot be located in history, but we still delight in them as an interesting alternative to our dreary, everyday lives. According to this option, literary writers supplement our weak imaginative faculty, which unfortunately assigns us only life in this world, with their own miraculously developed powerful imaginations.

But there is another way to understand the fabulous, which is at the core of Melville's understanding of literature as it is, perhaps, at the heart of all the great writers of the fabulous from Homer to Borges. According to this profound understanding, the three meanings of the fabulous come together when we locate the opening of the fabulous in the enigmatic realm of the white event of address, which for the novel is mainly defined as the encounter with the address of the white whale/wail at sea. We have seen that the white address that is the cry is an unbelievable and astonishing event which surprises the "I," and it is therefore fabulous in the first meaning of the term.

But as we have also seen, this white event that is the cry occurs in a realm prior to this or that stable meaning or identity, before the world has settled, and thus before a decision about the truth or falsity of this event of address can be made. As such the cry opens the trembling realm of fictionality, i.e. the second meaning of the term, as the realm where a decision about the reality of this event cannot yet be made, since one *does not know* what its meaning is, but only *that there is sense*, before this or that meaning. Thus fiction, before having to do with invention of non-existent beings and worlds, has to do with this diabolical[24] realm in which a decision about reality cannot yet be made

Third, I have suggested that this shadowy realm of the call has to do with the opening of time; as such it cannot itself be assigned a chronological location. Therefore, the cry opens a legendary and ahistorical realm not in the sense of some place outside time, but precisely as the event of time's opening. And thus it is fabulous in the third meaning of the term.

This event's fabulous nature should not be understood as offering some escapist fantasy from reality, for we have seen that the white event as the origin of the fabulous is also a disastrous, traumatic event. The collapse of the "I" involved in this event is a wounding devastation which destroys the "I"'s familiar and stable world. It is thus that the fabulous, the monstrous, and the disastrous open up together and are entangled in the same moment of address, linguistically associated with the cry.

It is the task of thinking further the nature of this fabulous cry, I suggest, which should constitute for our times the new locus from which to think literature.[25] For it signals a certain excess over every known traditional category that has attempted to define literature and art—as a beautiful object, a pleasing object, a fictional discourse, etc. Literature as a fabulous cry, as the fabulous language of testimony, or as an overwhelming and powerful white event that cannot be known but has to be transmitted, is in excess of itself, in excess of any known and stable identity that was ever assigned to it, and is drifting, orphaned, in search of a new destiny.

The sea and the life at sea, for the novel, and especially the life at sea exposed to the whales, when one experiences the world not as a collection of stable and recognizable objects but as an open realm of unknown and dangerous forces to which the helpless body is exposed and which it tries to manipulate and direct, is precisely an allegory of a way of life that is exposed to this fabulous and disastrous opening of language as a wail[26] before it has settled into landed, stable, and established meanings about which a judgment of truth can be made; and thus when language might still be said to have the value of rumor: "*[F]abulous rumors* naturally grow out of the very body of all *surprising terrible events* . . . but, in maritime life, far more than in that of terra firma, wild rumors abound, wherever there is any adequate reality for them to cling to. And as the sea surpasses the land in this matter, so the whale fishery surpasses every other sort of maritime life, in the *wonderfulness and fearfulness* of the rumors which sometimes circulate there. For not only are whalemen as a body unexempt from that ignorance and superstitiousness hereditary to all sailors; but of all sailors, they are by all odds the most directly brought into contact with whatever is *appallingly astonishing* in the sea; face to face they not only eye its greatest *marvels*, but, hand to jaw, give battle to them" (p. 180).

Moby-Dick and Literary History

Having thus defined *Moby-Dick* as a fabulous novel of testimony—and defined its challenge to our thinking about literature as precisely its posing the question of the literary as the encounter with a fabulous white cry—it might be the moment to digress a bit and raise the question of the relations between a book like *Moby-Dick* and literary history as well as the related question of whether it is possible to generalize from a singular book like *Moby-Dick* to something like Literature in general.

These issues, I suggest, have to be thought on mainly two levels. The first one can be called the conceptual or even logical level: *Moby-Dick* seems to me singular in having discovered, or perhaps more accurately in having exhaustively developed for the first time, the conceptual understanding of literary language as structured on an essential ambiguity between the language of the fabulous and the language of testimony, two languages which have been traditionally understood as opposed. A conceptual discovery, which, as we have seen, uncovers a certain event of address that is prior to the differentiation of fiction and reality. As such, *Moby-Dick* constitutes a break in literary history precisely by having most rigorously uncovered a conceptual logic that nevertheless can be generalized to all works of literature. In every work of literature, from the most fantastic to the most realistic, and even in seemingly documentary works, I suggest, the opening of language as a fabulous white cry is at the core, the essence of their character. Although more explicit in some works than in others, it nevertheless operates everywhere, and this is due to the fact of the strange contextlessness of literary language. For this language always comes to us without clear attribution and without a specific and specified addressee, a letter in a bottle, no matter how pressing or seductive is the historicist temptation to contextualize it.

But there is another, more complex level from which to think the generalizability of *Moby-Dick* and its relation to literary history, and it is also a more complex level from which to think the question of generalizability. This second level has to do with *Moby-Dick* as a singular address whose task it is to testify to, and transmit, a certain overwhelming event, a transmission that can only occur, as I've suggested in the introduction, as the performance of a work of literature or art.

We would thus first have to ask what is the event or events to which *Moby-Dick* testifies and which it performs? We might think, for example, of the Nantucket whaling ship *Essex*, wrecked by a sperm whale, whose tragic story inspired Melville. But we may also think of the extinction of the Pequod tribe, which Melville commemorates in his naming of *Moby-Dick*'s doomed ship. We might also think of the American black slaves and of other victims of the categories of race, to which *Moby-Dick* alludes through the figure of the black boy Pip, through its scathing critique of the imperialist investment in isolating and demarcating whiteness, and through its critical examination of the rhetoric and motivations of nineteenth century anatomical discourses.[27]

Thinking beyond these immediate historical contexts we might suggest, for example, that *Moby-Dick* testifies to a whole history of Western literature, from the Bible and the *Odyssey*, to Shakespeare, to Coleridge, since obviously all these works play a major role in the novel. In an even more strange and enigmatic way, as I have suggested in the introduction, *Moby-Dick* might be said to testify *avant-la-lettre* to the horrors of the disasters and catastrophes of the twentieth century and to twentieth century writers such as Artaud and Celan.

What would it mean to say that *Moby-Dick* testifies to all these events that seem to belong to varying historical contexts and constitute very different kind of events (i.e. are "literary" or "historical"), and how can we think the strange logic that unites them or makes them, through *Moby-Dick*, communicate with each other, and in a way testify to each other?

Testimony as the novel understands it, I have been arguing in this book, is not a report on a knowledge unavailable to others that is supposed to be authenticated by a judge, but rather the passive, forced, and unwilling submission to the wounding of an incomprehensible and overwhelming white event whose status is neither true or false but that of an address prior to these possibilities. This submission truly becomes an act of witnessing only through the transformation of the passive receiver into the active performer and transmitter of the event. The white event cannot and should not be transformed into knowledge—and thus in principle cannot be authenticated by a judge—but *exists only* in its transmission or communication from one witness to another and so forth.

Not being able to know and understand the event, and essentially so, means that the event cannot be reduced to its context or to any context. This failure of knowledge and understanding *uncovers an essentially uncontextualizable dimension*, that is, a dimension that cannot be reduced to causal explanations that locate the event in a specific historical time and place that is supposed to provide the conditions of possibility for the event's occurrence. The white event in its absolute surprise is precisely disastrous in that it essentially undermines any contextualizing thought, any causal thought, thus any historicist thought which understands history as providing the conditions of possibility for the event.

We might thus see how the thought of the white event as the thought of disaster promises a new thought of history and a new thought of the relations between literature and history. That is, the concept of disaster should be understood as a *historical category*. It is a concept that complicates and puts into question the primacy given in more traditional literary studies to the notion of historical context, in relation to which the literary work's historicity is usually understood. The disaster, along with the absolute surprise and shock it brings forth, is precisely the destruction of context, the annihilation of any framework through which the horrible white event can be explained, and thus explained away. The literary work, I claim, is the linguistic event that is dedicated to preserving—in the sense of "bearing witness to, which is essentially also a communicative performance of"— the "disastrous" quality of any significant event, that is, to the impossibility of reducing it to a specific historical context. It is precisely because the literary work preserves this disastrous and contextless dimension that literary works from even very distant pasts may speak to us at all, and *address us*. For *only* at the moment when a certain event cannot be completely assimilated to and explained by its specific historical context does a need for a future arise, in the shape of an addressee, who will respond to what the present cannot answer. History thus opens as a call or address of that incomprehensible event which cannot be assimilated to a present context, and *literature as a historical discourse* opens as that whose task it is to transmit this excess over the present, which opens the future.

We can now come back to the question of the nature of

Moby-Dick's witnessing to the historical and literary events that I have sketched above. Claiming that *Moby-Dick* testifies to the *Odyssey* and the Bible, to the genocide of the American Indians and to the disaster of the *Essex* (and this list could be infinitely extended, since not only does it include the past but in a way the future as well) means that it responds to something in these events that is a white and incomprehensible enigma, which exceeds any possible explanation of their arrival. It also means that these events will continue to exist as real events, i.e. white events, only if they survive as literary events, that is, as events that testify to the incomprehensible excess of these historical occurrences through their performance, a performance which opens the future as that which must respond to the incomprehensibility of these events. Only in this way are these events not simply remnants of the past, to be historicistically catalogued, but are addressed to us in our own present and "context," and beyond it, opening our future.

It is precisely in this remaining open of the enigmatic past beyond its own context that these historical events communicate and resonate even with chronologically "later" events—the destruction of the Indians is linked to the disaster of the Jews, for example—and thus a book like *Moby-Dick* can be said to testify to twentieth-century events, that is, to speak for them and to communicate the horrible excess beyond linear historical time which was revealed through their occurrence. It is because of this that there is no essential difference between *Moby-Dick*'s testifying to "literary" events and its testifying to "historical" events. Both kinds of events actually address us in a similar manner, they are horrifying, disastrous events in which something happens that destroys our capacity for understanding, and they both can be said to exist as white events only in the work of literature which testifies to them and performs them, transmitting them to the future.

This logic demands as well a new understanding of the way a singular work such as *Moby-Dick* might be generalized and speaks for something like the wider "category" of literature. If science, at least as it is traditionally understood, deduces laws from a limited number of experiments or observation of events and generalizes from them to a much wider, in principle infinite, number of events, the laws themselves presumed to have always pertained to these events even before their formulations as laws, then literary generalizability is of a completely different nature. Literary generalizability in the more profound sense (that is, beyond the simply logical-conceptual formalization of its type of language as fabulous/testimonial), I argue, has to be performed; it cannot be assumed to have existed prior to its performance. That is, if literature involves the witnessing to a singular disastrous event which it has to transmit, and which exists only in this transmission, then, as I have argued in the introduction, in order for this singularity to continue to exist one cannot simply know about it, but one has to participate in it, become witness to it/actor of it. That is, the singular event *can* be generalized, or even universalized, that is, pertain to every single member of humanity, but not as something that can be presumed to pertain a priori to everyone or to anyone, but rather as something that addresses everyone and calls them to perform it, to participate in its occurrence.

Thus if a singular event like *Moby-Dick*, or any other literary work for that matter, is to be generalizable, speak for something, or rather as something, like "literature in general," then it cannot do so as an individual case speaking for a general law. Rather, it has to establish itself as a witness to the whole history of Western literature, whose existence and survival as the keeper and guard of this horrible excess of numerous wounding white events which communicate with each other through it, depend each time on the coming into being of a witness which will transmit its historical address to the future. But in an even more complex manner, *Moby-Dick*'s establishing itself as a singular witness that nevertheless speaks as the whole of Western literature requires that the entire body of Western literature, in a way, be understood as testifying to *Moby-Dick*, that is, as responding to its event, being wounded, or marked by it, transformed by it, and transmitting itself henceforth as carrying on its skin *Moby-Dick*'s white and enigmatic scar.

Thus the generalizability of any literary event depends on this double movement of testifying to a disastrous event or wound. That is, on the one hand, the movement of carrying on its body the wound of history and transmitting the disaster to which this literary history testified, and on the other hand, transmitting itself through a wounding of this history. It is only through this *generalizable performative force*, which is the force of transmitting one's being wounded by history back into history, forcing it to testify in its turn to this new event, that a new literary witness can come into being and become a member of what is called—in a way which completely erases the violence of the event—the literary tradition.[28]

Moby-Dick is a work particularly and acutely aware of this logic, and hence its encyclopedic quality, encompassing as it does numerous texts from all periods of Western writing. This encyclopedic quality should not (at least not only) be understood as the ravenous drive to swallow the entire corpus of Western writing—although it is also that, according to the complex double logic that I have shown to operate in both Ahab and Ishmael—

but rather, and especially, it should be grasped as an awareness of its role to witness the whole of literary history and transmit it to the future, a role that can only be fulfilled if literary history in its entirety testifies to it, transformed and wounded by it. Thus what has been called intertextuality, that is, the presence of foreign textual fragments within the body of particular literary works, proves itself to be essentially a category of witnessing. What these foreign textual fragments bring is not some new and wider contexts to aid the interpretation of the literary work, but rather the presence of a decontextualized excess that marks the body of the text with a foreign wound to which it testifies, and which marks in its turn the body of the fragment's source text with the mark of the later text.

This logic seems to me to complicate such a well-known historical logic as Harold Bloom's conception of the anxiety of influence. The drama played out between the "tradition" and any "strong" newcomer is not an Oedipal drama (or not only), but more profoundly, a drama of witnessing where the newcomer witnesses/acts the tradition, which can only happen if the tradition witnesses/acts the newcomer's wounding event. The newcomer should be understood as exactly that, as the one whose arrival is absolutely new and unforeseen, an absolute surprise, a surprise witness who is the only one able to testify to the unforeseen excess kept alive only within literary history.

Paradoxically, it is in order to become a witness to literary history, meaning a witness to the disastrous wound, or wail, which resonates in it, perhaps unbeknownst to it, that *Moby-Dick* in particular, and perhaps nineteenth-century American literature in general, has to *separate* itself from this history, has to become an absolutely new beginning.[29] Like Ishmael's witnessing of Ahab, which involves a radical separation from his drive, so do all acts of witnessing, including *Moby-Dick's* witnessing of literary history, involve a *radical act of separation*, an act of freedom in regard to the drive of history, the only act allowing a witnessing to that which in history exceeds history, or at least exceeds history understood as a series of causal events.

Ishmael: Whale-Author(ity)

Let us now return to our examination of Ishmael and his capacity as whale-author(ity). As I have mentioned, Ishmael's sea narrative can be roughly divided into two parts: the main story line, in which he more or less participates, and which follows the adventures of the whalemen, those whose lives are exposed to the whales at sea, and an alternating whale-narrative, investigating and responding to the enigma of the whale, that keeps interrupting the main story line which is mostly dominated and driven by Ahab's murderous hunt. Our discussion of the extraordinarily rich aspect of Ishmael as the narrator of the sea will limit itself to two main issues: 1) we will first inquire briefly into Ishmael's narrative logic and rhetorical strategies by mainly concentrating on his extremely ambiguous whale narrative. 2) We will then inquire into the various functions that this narrative might be said to entertain in relation to the main story line.

The various rhetorical positions that Ishmael takes in his whale-narrative and whalemen's-narrative mainly elaborate on and develop the implications of the basic positions I have delineated above, implications derived from the logic of the white event. I will therefore limit myself to a few concrete examples.

The white event, we have seen, is an overwhelming event that exhausts the capacities of the one undergoing it, brings about the collapse of the language of knowledge, and constitutes the ambiguous figure of an investigator of the enigma of the event/witness to this event, always in the position of an accused having to prove his/her testimony that is not available to everyone/fabulist—both in the sense of someone attempting to persuade of very implausible and false claims and someone whose discourse resorts to the legendary, the fictional and the ahistorical. We have also seen that the discourse of the witness of whiteness ambiguously moves between a proliferating, open discourse which courageously and movingly refuses to close the excess of whiteness and lets it be heard behind every meaning, and a discourse of mastery, driven by a possessive desire to write over whiteness. Ishmael's whale-narrative moves ambiguously among these positions.

Let us start by taking a brief look at the two chapters that can be said to open Ishmael's adventure as the narrator and storyteller of the whalemen and of the whale, chapters that set the tone for much of what follows: These chapters are chapter 24—"the Advocate," the chapter that marks the transition from the "landish" part of the novel to its sea part, and the famous chapter 32, "Cetology."

As if making an opening statement to the distinguished members of some jury, taking the role of the advocate (or is it playing the devil's[30] advocate?), in a mixture of the (hyperbolic? feigned? melodramatic? or real and deeply affecting?) pathos of the wrongfully accused and the confidence of someone resolutely bringing incontestable and irrefutable evidence, Ishmael argues (in the chapter "The Advocate") the unlikely case of the whalemen and of the whale itself becoming the main subject of a book. The whalemen are more or less credited for everything that is good and pure, from curing cancer to world peace, and the whale itself is presented as the noblest and best subject a writer could ever wish to approach, more beautiful than Helen of Troy and more entertaining than Groucho Marx.

Doubtless one leading reason why the world declines honoring us whalemen, is this: they think that, at best, our vocation amounts to a butchering sort of business; and that when actively engaged therein, we are surrounded by all manners of defilements. . . .

But, though the world scouts at us whale hunters, yet does it unwittingly pay us the profoundest homage; yea, an all-abounding adoration! for almost all the tapers, lamps, and candles that burn round the globe, burn, as before so many shrines, to our glory! . . .

But this is not the half; look again.

I freely assert, that the cosmopolite philosopher cannot, for his life, point out one single peaceful influence, which within the last sixty years has operated more potentially upon the whole broad world, taken in one aggregate, than the high and mighty business of whaling. . . .

it might be distinctly shown how from those whalemen at last eventuated the liberation of Peru, Chili and Bolivia from the yoke of Old Spain and the establishment of the eternal democracy in those parts. . . .

But if, in the face of all this, you still declare that whaling has no aesthetically noble associations connected with it, then am I ready to shiver fifty lances with you there, and unhorse you with a split helmet every time.

The whale has no famous author, and the whaling no famous chronicler, you will say. *The whale no famous author, and whaling no famous chronicler?* [italics in original.] Who wrote the first account of our Leviathan? Who but mighty Job! And who composed the first narrative of a whaling-voyage? Who, but no less a prince than Alfred the Great, who, with his own royal pen, took down the words from Other, the Norwegian whale-hunter of those times! (pp. 108–11)

Continuing in this vein, Ishmael accumulates one on top of the other the qualities of, and arguments for, the incomparable and unique whale and the unparalleled whalemen's life.

But, although Ishmael the lawyer can be said to be a witness arguing for, and bringing into light, the unheard-of and unacknowledged revolutionary and liberating voice of the whale and of the whalemen/a fabulous rhetorician who can sell ice to the Eskimos, he is also the one whose speech brings to light, on the one hand, the unacknowledged sound of a murderous adventure, and on the other hand performs a murder. A murder that has to do both with his language's desire to possess the audience (which is also the whalemen's imperialistic desire to possess the world and to reach every uncharted place) and with the equalizing nature of the language of the law itself; a language, as we have briefly seen, which can be said by definition to stifle the singular and destabilizing whale/wail by turning it into an any whale whatsoever, a general "case" which is the only one acceptable in a court of law. Likewise, this legalistic type of equalizing characterizes the whale-industry itself that is said to serve as an "interpreter" between the white men and the "savages," thus reducing the plurality of languages into one language to ensure the reign of a global economic order and international law.

Thus the advocate provocatively admits: "Butchers we are, that is true. But butchers, also, and butchers of the bloodiest badge have been all Martial Commanders whom the world invariably delights to honor . . ." and, unwittingly bringing to light the murderous consequences and nature of the whalemen's adventures, he says: "For many years past the whale-ship has been the pioneer in ferreting out the remotest and least known parts of the earth. She has explored seas and archipelagoes which had no chart, where no Cook and Vancouver had ever sailed. If American and European men-of-war now peacefully ride in once savage harbors, let them fire salutes to the honor and the glory of the whale-ship, which originally showed them the way, and first interpreted between them and the savages" (p. 110).

Chapter 32—"Cetology," or the science of whales, is the chapter in which Ishmael's whale-narrative really begins. This very long chapter demands (as do most chapters of this exhaustingly demanding novel[31]), and has partially received, an extended reading.[32] Yet for our present purposes I will limit myself to a few points.

> Already we are boldly launched upon the deep; but soon we shall be *lost* in its *unshored*, harborless immensities. Ere that come to pass; ere the Pequod's weedy hull rolls side by side with the barnacled hulls of the leviathan; at the outset it is but well to attend to a matter almost indispensable to a thorough appreciative understanding of the more special leviathanic revelations and allusions of all sorts which are to follow.
>
> It is some *systematized* exhibition of the whale in his broad genera, that I would now fain put before you. Yet is it no easy task. The *classification* of the constituents of a chaos, nothing less is here essayed. Listen to what the best and latest *authorities* have laid down . . . (p. 134)

The very same ambiguities that we have seen operating in the analytic chapter on whiteness operate in this analytic or scientific chapter as well. Without repeating my analysis of the various functions of the analytic language and the various voices of the investigator (stammering witness, diabolical fabulist trying to persuade, eager scientist, etc.) I will mention that the very logic of this ambiguity derives here as well from the unmasterable, unclassifiable, unshored, and unsystematizable nature of the whale as a white event, which undermines and destabilizes any authority trying to take hold of it.

Among the various reasons (or alternatively pseudo-reasons)

given for the failures of science, of cognitive grasping, in the case of the whale, a science that, Ishmael initially hopes, might be finally brought to a satisfying conclusion with him, as if chosen by the whale to be its scientific witness, is the fact that almost none of the whale scientists was ever *witness to the living* whale, and *only one* could really speak of the whale from within a certain *living experience of the event of whaling*: "Of the names in this list of *whale authors*, only those following Owen ever saw living whales; and but one of them was a real professional harpooner and whaleman. I mean Captain Scoresby. On the separate subject of Greenland or right-whale, he is the best existing authority" (p. 135). Thus, if there is to be a science of the (living) whale, it will be a strange science, which demands the passionate involvement of the subject of investigation with that which is investigated.

Yet even this single authority of whales that was Scoresby has not witnessed the sperm whale, which remained "*fabulous* or utterly unknown" (p. 135) and until now, "the sperm whale, scientific or poetic, *lives not complete in any literature*. Far above all other hunted whales, his is an *unwritten life*" (p. 135). But this is about to change, claims Ishmael, the sperm-whale's life can finally be witnessed, "the time has at last come for a new proclamation" (p. 135). Yet, in erecting this hitherto unachieved system through which the life of the whale can truly be witnessed, Ishmael, time and again, seems to fail.[33] The whale cannot really be systematized, for even if he has managed to deal with "all the Leviathans of note" there still remains "a rabble of uncertain, fugitive, *half-fabulous* whales, which, as an American whaleman, *I know by reputation, but not personally*" (p. 144). Reports of still more "uncertain whales" he suspects are but "mere sounds, full of Leviathanism, but signifying nothing" (p. 145) for he himself has not witnessed them, but merely found references in some "Icelandic, Dutch, and old English *authorities*" (p. 145). This is a very strange science indeed, where the authority of the testimony of another stands under an essential suspicion of fabulation.[34] Why should we, in our turn, accept Ishmael's testimony, which by claiming its status as a sole witness also demands we accept his authority without opportunity to defend our suspicions?

An essential remainder of fabulous rumors and of the impossibility of witnessing, and also an essential demand for a personal witnessing, thus seem to block the possibility of the fully grasping the whale and its life. Thus, finally, Ishmael has to admit his failure: "But I now leave my cetological System standing thus unfinished, even as the great Cathedral of Cologne was left, with the crane still standing upon the top of the uncompleted tower"[35] (p. 145).

This double collapse of any investigation of the whale into the fabulous and into a demand for personal witnessing recurs in various modes during Ishmael's whale narrative (in the form of a collapse of all the sciences, a collapse of historical investigation, and even a collapse of the possibility for story-telling, etc.). Yet it might be that this collapse, which, I argue, is the collapse into wailing and crying, is the very form through which this novel attempts to transmit and reverberate its white event of wounding and disaster that is the whale/wail and its life. And yet this collapse might also be just one more strategy on the part of devious Ishmael the lawyer to emotionally manipulate his jury (i.e. us, the readers) into believing his preposterous argument by displaying a feigned weakness that discourages us to look further into his claims. This essential and constitutive either/or is, I have been trying to prove, the very essence of the white event of address, and you have to take my word for it, for embarking on such an investigation is no easy matter, and it took three years of my life.

Let me quickly give one more example of this collapse into the fabulous and into the demand for a personal and singular event of witnessing, this time dealing with the collapse of aesthetic representation. In the paradoxically titled and highly ironic Chapter 55—"Of the Monstrous Pictures of Whales"[36] Ishmael takes it upon himself to criticize all previous attempts to represent the whale,[37] while he, on the other hand, "shall ere long paint to you as well as one can without canvas, something like the *true* form of the whale as he actually appears to the eye of the whaleman when in his own absolute body the whale is moored alongside the whale-ship so that he can be fairly stepped upon there" (p. 260).

All the previous pictures of the whale are termed "imaginary portraits" and "pictorial *delusions*"[38] (p. 260), and some of them indeed represent a "very picturesque but purely *fabulous* creature, imitated, I take it, from the like figures on antique vases"[39] (p. 261). He also harshly criticizes those pictures of the leviathan "purporting to be sober, scientific, delineations, by *those who know*" (pp. 261–62).

In short, "these manifold mistakes in depicting the whale are not so very surprising after all," for "though elephants have stood for their full-lengths, the *living* Leviathan has never yet fairly floated himself for his portrait. The *living whale*, in his full majesty and significance, is only to be seen at sea in unfathomable waters." That is, none of its painters ever really endured the event of its encounter, and thus "you must needs conclude that the great Leviathan is that one creature in the world which *must remain unpainted to the last.*" For "there is no earthly way of finding out precisely what the whale really looks like. And the *only mode in which you can derive even a tolerable idea of his living contour, is by going whaling yourself;* but by so doing, you run no small risk of being eternally stove and sunk by him. Wherefore, *it seems to me you had best not be too fastidious in your curiosity touching this Leviathan*"[40] (pp. 263–64).

Thus the whale collapses any mastery of representation and is that which can only be witnessed by a "me"[41] exposed to its life, while any other representation of it is always suspected of fabulation, delusion, and monstrous deformation. But what about Ishmael's discourse, how should we therefore listen to it? Is it exempt from its own rules?

Perhaps the chapter most crucial to the success of the mission and task, perhaps even the calling, of Ishmael the whale-author (besides the chapter "The Whiteness of the Whale"[42]) is Chapter 45, "The Affidavit."[43] in which the very question of the truth of the whale as disaster is at stake. Trying to persuade his listeners of the "natural verity of the main points of this affair [i.e. the disaster]" (p. 203) and to defend against vicious accusations that his testimony to it is not real but fabricated, Ishmael says: "I do not know where I can find a better place than just here, to make mention of one or two other things, which to me seem important, as in printed form establishing in all respects the *reasonableness* of the whole story of the White Whale, more especially the *catastrophe*. For this is one of those disheartening instances where truth requires full as much bolstering as error. So ignorant are most landsmen of some of the plainest and most palpable wonders of the world, that without some hints touching the plain facts, historical and otherwise of the fishery, they might scout at Moby Dick as a *monstrous fable*, or still worse and more detestable, a hideous and intolerable allegory" (p. 205).

Yet, to persuade us of the veracity of his account, and of the non-fabulous, or monstrous, nature of his testimony, Ishmael has to convince us of his reliability, and even his *authority as a witness*. Yet Ishmael finds no better method to achieve this than to rely on the authority of other witnesses to events of disaster which he did not himself witness: "But fortunately the special point I here seek can be established upon *testimony entirely independent of my own*." The list of these testimonies is varied, starting from a supposedly completely accurate historical testimony, with a reference to an exact date, a name, and a place ("In the year 1820 the ship Essex, Captain Pollard, of Nantucket, was cruising in the Pacific Ocean . . ." [p. 206]) and ending with a citation, taken from what sounds more like fabulous history, from one sixth-century writer Procupius whose authority as a witness itself has to be established by the fact that "[b]y the best *authorities*, he has always been considered a most trustworthy and unexaggerating historian, *except* in some one or two particulars" which are, Ishmael claims confidently, "not at all affecting the matter presently to be mentioned" (p. 209).

Yet even this Procupius talks in his "historical" writings only of some sea-monster that destroyed ships in the sea of Maramara over some fifty years, a monster that Ishmael, at first, confidently, claims "must have been a whale" (p. 210) (although there don't seem to be whales in the sea of Maramara, but perhaps there could have been, for Ishmael was told "on good authority" (p. 210) that someone found a skeleton of a whale in the Mediterranean, and it is therefore likely that, perhaps, a whale could also reach the sea of Maramara, if it managed to pass through the Dardanelles). Finally, Ishmael ends the chapter somewhat less confidently when he states that "Procupius' sea-monster . . . must *in all probability* have been a sperm whale" (p. 210).

Thus, in order to somehow manage to prove his point, not

only does Ishmael in this chapter have to betray the very principles that he himself set according to which his own personal witnessing is the only trustworthy criterion for the authority of his testimony to the whale. All of a sudden, he trusts other authorities which earlier were suspected of fabulous and monstrous deformations, but which he now, for some reason, judges to be "reliably known to me"[44] (p. 203). What's more, the very authorities upon which he relies slip unnoticeably from a supposedly referential-historical discourse to fabulous and legendary tales about sea-monsters.[45]

The disaster of the whale, this traceless white event (for everyone but Ishmael died and their remains and the ship were lost at sea[46]) witnessed, if it indeed happened, *only by one* abandoned survivor incapable of producing proof, collapses as we have seen, every possibility of external authority to corroborate the event, and even the possibility of an internal authority; for the white event of disaster means that I become a white and monstrous riddle to myself, and I cannot therefore even say for sure that the disaster actually happened. No one bears witness for the witness,[47] says Paul Celan, and this is indeed the inevitable consequence of the white event.[48]

Yet Ishmael's endeavors in this chapter, trying as he does to prove the truth of the disaster's existence, seem to involve a refusal of this law of the witness (of the white event) by, precisely, his attempt to bring a witness for the witness. Bringing a witness for the witness means restoring authority, an authority that had been lost with the singular white event. This restoration of authority (or of pseudo-authority), which is both external and internal, is demanded by Ishmael's positions as scientist, advocate, and witness seeking to restore reason/fabulist trying to convince his audience of the authority of his tale. His resort to other authorities to prove his disastrous and monstrous claims thus seems to serve the double function of both corroborating his authority as a witness in the face of an audience, and to proving even to himself that it is indeed possible that he endured that which he feels and claims to have undergone.

Yet restoring authority from within its collapse and extreme limit in the white event of disaster proves to be a very strange and paradoxical task. The very peculiar and seemingly arbitrary use Ishmael makes of authority in this chapter, involving the lack of distinction between what sounds like referential-historical authority and what sounds like fabulous legend, as well as with the quite obvious fact that it is he who finally authorizes the validity of the authorities he uses that will, in their turn, authorize him; this use of authority, by uncovering several of authority's presuppositions, suggests that the logic of authority itself is no less problematic and complex than that of the white event, and that it indeed constitutes itself first and foremost in relation to the white event. Going even further, we might say that the logic of authority strangely mimics that of the white event, is constantly haunted by it and threatened by it as its spectral double, and originates and collapses in relation to it. Perhaps the uncovering of the relations between the thought of authority and the thought of the white event will expose us to a different kind of authority, or even to something that is different from authority altogether. Let us see how.

Ishmael's attempt to recuperate authority in relation to the disaster, authority understood as authority over the truth or fictiveness of the event, exposes the two-sided nature of authority. On the one hand, it seems to be caught in an infinite regression in which no authority can stand alone but always needs other authorities to authorize it. On the other hand, and this inevitably follows from the first point, if authority always depends on another authority, a first authority would have had to have been established which is unauthorized, that is, which is arbitrary, laid down like a law, and which could somehow stop this infinite regression. Thus, if the white event meant that there is no witness for the witness, from the point of view of authority a similar structure is exposed where there is finally no authority for authority. And this arbitrary institution of authority is most crucially called for precisely in relation to the threat of the white event.

Thus, finally, after all of Ishmael's attempts to find support in other authorities, the authority of which, as I have said, he himself needed to authorize, his claims come down to this: my testimony is authoritative because I say so.[49] I authorize or legislate my own and others' authority to witness, and arbitrarily so, I am the advocate arguing for a law which I myself have written down. I am the one deciding what is for truth and what for fiction, and I therefore tell you, and you must take my word for it, that what I say actually happened. I can therefore use what sounds like referential history and what sounds like fabulous legend in the same way, for I am the one who, finally, decides what is history and what is legend.

Ishmael thus seems to recuperate his loss of authority over his own experience, a loss that resulted from the disastrous address of the whale, by arbitrarily asserting the validity of his own testimony as well as those of others. From this point of view, Ishmael attempts to establish himself as the absolute sovereign and author(ity), of himself, of the text, and of us the readers.

Yet this discovery of the ultimately arbitrary nature of Ishmael's authority to bear witness only begins to complicate the question of authority involved in our reading of the book; for obviously, there is also another, specularly symmetrical, side to this attempt of Ishmael to establish himself as master of truth and fiction. This other side has to do with the absolute helplessness with which he, finally, stands before us, the readers, an accused exposed to our judgment. For the text, as a literary text, in opposition to a real sovereign, has no real legislative authority over us, and there is no reason that we should find its authority binding. It could exercise no real power over us, it lacks the force that must always accompany authority as its shadow and which, finally, is the only real self-founding authority.[50]

It would therefore seem that authority is in our hands, that we are the truly authoritative judges and masters who can decide as we wish about Ishmael's authority and about the truth or fiction of his testimony. Yet our reception of *Moby-Dick* as a work of literature, and thus presumably fiction, also exposes the helplessness of our own authority, since it is not we who decided its status, but, probably, some other authority that has proclaimed that this is a work of fiction for us in advance. But the work itself, trying to wrest itself free of the grip of external authorities and to instituting itself as master by symbolically declaring its independence from every external authority through its status as a sole witness, seems to demand at the same time that the reader not rely on these external authorities, in fact encourages the reader to rebel against them by collaborating with the work, and actually institute himself or herself as a master of truth and fiction who can make claims about the institutionalized work of fiction thus: this is truth speaking, for I, with my own authority, judge the testimony of the book to be true and not fiction, I declare myself a privileged witness to its revelation of truth, and I will use my force and violence to institute my own authority to authorize the text as a proof of my authority.[51]

And thus, the question again arises whether the text itself authorized me to authorize it, or whether I authorized the text to authorize me. And so forth: infinite mirror play of the regression of authority and the self-institutionalization of authority opens up before us, where it can finally never be clear whose authority has instituted itself and whose is derived, for even in the case of one who is presumed to have the last, and therefore first, word, through his/her capacity for violence, it cannot be clear whether he/she used force in their own name, or in the name of an other which speaks through them, perhaps unbeknownst to them.[52]

It is precisely at this point that the white event of disaster can be said to infiltrate authority, destroy it from within, and make it collapse. For there always remains at the heart of authority as self-instituting violence the suspicion that something preceded it, a certain call or address that called authority to itself and in relation to which authority instituted itself, yet which it can never itself master nor authorize as hard as it tries; and it is thus that authority feels most at risk and has to institute itself the most violently and arbitrarily in relation to any event, or possible event, of address. Authority, at its extreme limit, becomes a white riddle to itself, and the call thus marks the unauthorized, monstrous impotence at its heart and the principle of its resistance.

Thus, from within this terrible noise made by all the authorities and forces collapsing and trying to recuperate themselves as masters, battling over the status of the text as truth or fiction,[53] something else altogether can be heard, something which is, precisely, a white noise, an addressed white whale/wail. The white event of disaster which is at the heart of the text seems to have exposed the mechanism of authority to a blind spot, a turbulent vortex, a yawning gulf, which no authority can overcome and into which they all collapse.[54]

But this collapse, I suggest, can become the revolutionary moment that calls for a new understanding of authority, or for something different from authority altogether, for a new understanding of fiction or the fabulous, and for a new understanding of witnessing. For it is perhaps out of this general collapse (of Ishmael and of the reader as knowledgeable authorities over the text, along with that of any other political and literary establishment's knowledgeable authority) that Ishmael's white whale/wail is actually heard, that the life of the whale/wail can actually be witnessed, that his testimony becomes, in a way, authoritative, but not in the sense of an epistemic authority arbitrating the knowledge of truth and fiction,[55] nor in the sense of something which the text, separate from me, authoritatively possesses and commands to me, but through an overwhelming, white event, which no authority can ever guarantee in advance or stabilize, happening in between the text and me, which all of a sudden imposes itself on me and as a consequence of which I find myself having to ask not "Is Ishmael telling the truth or not? Can I trust his authority or not? Did the disaster actually happen or not? Does the whale exist or not?" but rather "What happened to me? What all of a sudden imposed itself on me so powerfully (and authoritatively?) that I discover that who I am is at stake, for I don't know anymore, and I find myself having to answer for who I am, and having been chosen despite myself to witness this white whale/wail revealed to me, perhaps,[56] through my collapse, which tells me that I must do something, but not what to do, and which I have to reverberate into the future, not in the sense of stating for the sake of the future that it is true that this white whale/wail of which the text speaks actually happened, but precisely by becoming myself a white wail, a white cry, an event through which a wound is performed and transmitted, not as truth[57] but as an enigmatic scar."[58]

That is, the authority of witnessing has to be thought anew (or perhaps it is something different from authority), not as a stable and established authority over truth and fiction (which always carries the mark of arbitrariness and violence), but as the *authority of the event, an authority that happens* and is not decided upon from the stable and distant vantage of the land. Authority in this new understanding is not in the possession of any authority, is never guaranteed, it is also an unauthorized authority, but not in the sense of an arbitrary and violent unauthorization that can remain a stable principle, but in the sense of something that imposes itself surprisingly on me from within itself, something that happens to a "me" but does not institute itself, and leaves no proof of its existence.[59]

We can thus say that the disaster might have actually happened, but if it happened and is witnessed to by the text (which is never certain), it is not witnessed in the form of some distant event which occurred in the past that allows the text, and its reader, to assume a masterful position of the one who knows and of the purveyor of truth, a sole survivor safe on land. If the disaster indeed happened, and is to be witnessed, it must involve an explosion of time. It must also be happening right now.[60]

It is within this strange space opened by the text, or more accurately in between the text and me, and a "me," that the disaster is happening, a space between the fabulous and the testimonial, which are now no longer understood as the field of forces over which authorities of truth and fiction are battling, but are the names for a powerful and enigmatic white wail whose status is neither true nor fictional, but that of an event of address located before them.[61]

Literature, understood now as the taking place, the witnessing, and the "performance" of this possible powerful white disaster, thus becomes, or perhaps is discovered to have always been, the fabulous opening of language before truth or falsity, that which puts into question and problematizes the logic of authority and the legal conceptualization which comes with it, and as a consequence is beyond, or in excess of, every "external" discourse trying to dominate it, judge it, and authorize it, and thus in excess of literature, understood as a stable identity.

From the perspective of our discussion of the double nature of authority we can also understand the double nature of the recourse to the vocabulary of power in the novel. In its more profound and enigmatic form the vocabulary of power in the novel has to be thought in relation to the white event. Indeed, we might say that the thought of power for the novel is exactly the thought of whiteness; *power imposes as whiteness* and is called for precisely in the same way as whiteness, with all the various issues we have associated with it (which obviously include the thought of language as cry and of the body as wound). But there is another language of power in the novel, associated with the tyrannical and the authoritarian hunt for the stable land. This language of power, the stabilizing and violent one, is to be understood as constituting itself in relation to, originating from, and collapsing in the encounter with, the white language of power, trying to mimic it and destroy it.[62]

Having examined several of the complexities and ambiguities involved in Ishmael's whale investigations, let me head toward conclusion by briefly suggesting the functions they might be said to entertain in relation to the main story-line, dominated by Ahab's whale/wail with its shattering pathos and murderous drive, which they constantly interrupt. For it seems to me that it is the opening up of the difference between these two narratives and the relations between them that constitutes the model for any event of true witnessing, and thus for any event of true reading, as it is understood by the novel.

I have said that a white difference that opened between Ahab and Ishmael allowed Ishmael his freedom from Ahab's possessive drive, a white difference that involved nothing but apprehending Ahab as a white event, an addressed enigma in which who he is, is at stake. I would therefore argue that Ishmael's alternating and alternative narrative is first of all the opening up of a new destiny through this enigma, a destiny separate from that of Ahab, and freed from it. Yet this freedom is not to be understood as an unrelated, willful separation from Ahab's destiny, but it is precisely *a freedom opened up and called for by Ahab's destiny*. That which calls from within Ahab's destiny is Ahab's white wail of life (and the sailors wail of life, and the whale's wail of life), which resists being hunted down by Ahab's authoritarian dream and desire for mastery, and which all of a sudden imposes itself on Ishmael as a white and enigmatic address demanding to be witnessed, investigated, responded to, and reverberated by Ishmael's life.

Indeed, I would argue that speech itself, in the profound sense of the word, is originated and is born through a "me" being thus moved by the others' cry of pathos, the wounds of their lives, which demand to be witnessed and reverberated against any totalitarian mastery. *Speaking means being moved to speak*, and it opens up as a freedom to speak and as a principle of resistance not in the sense in which I can say what I wish to say when no one is able or allowed to bother me, but in the sense that through it a white event of freedom is opened and a separate destiny can come to be through which the cry that calls for witnessing can be responded to. The white event of literature is thus that which opens speech as a movement to speak and a freedom to speak, and literature can now be understood as the bringing about, the happening of, the birth of language in the reader as a wail, each time for the first time, through becoming a witness to/performer of a disaster.

Ahab's, the sailors', and the whale's destiny, all of which occupies the main narrative, could therefore only be witnessed if a new, alternative destiny is open, a path that resists Ahab's drive and its narrative and frees the wail of life hunted down by it. The wail is thus witnessed in the space of freedom, opened in-between the main story-line and Ishmael's alternative narrative of whale investigation. Speaking from the point of view of the reader, if the main story-line is dominated by Ahab's drive, it is also dominated by the reader's drive for satisfaction that this suspenseful narrative of revenge creates. Ishmael's alternative whale narrative, notoriously cumbersome and boring at times, interrupts this drive of the reader and attempts to expose him/her to another whale, the white wail heard in the white spaces occupying the in-between of the alternating narratives. This interruption can also be said to intensify the drive because it frustrates the desire to get back to the hunt, and thus exposes it to the hunt's murderous quality. But it can also be said to create a stronger, more murderous drive. How is whiteness to be witnessed without right away being possessed by a new drive?

For indeed, if Ishmael's alternating narrative opens up a new destiny it also opens up also a new drive and desire, which, as we have seen, is at times no less murderous than Ahab's bloody hunt. Ishmael's adventure, although being a reverberation of and testimony to Ahab's adventure, becomes, in its turn, a repetition of Ahab's murderous adventure, a repetition which the reader, being called as he/she is by the white wail resonating in the novel, has to resist and interrupt by opening a new destiny of witnessing, investigating, and reverberating. But the reader's destiny, of course, is itself guilty of creating a new kind of murderous desire, which, in its turn, will have to be resisted, and the cry freed again. It is perhaps only in the space of interruption between all these various destinies, tied as they are to each other, and separate as they are from each other, that the white wail can, at least momentarily, be heard.

Coda

And what this almost inaudible cry says—a fabulous white wail of pathos which can suddenly overwhelm in any event of encounter and to which the work of literature, more than any other speech-event, is dedicated—is the following: Be witness to my life and to my death, for I have chosen you to be my witness, call me by my name and bring me to myself, remember me, keep telling my story, and be willing to make your life an echoing of my word. But also, transform and revolutionize your life, not by imitating me but by responding to my call or by responding to my life as to a call—leave your belongings, your home and the stable land in which you have grown, and come to sea.

But is this a false call? Is this a siren's song? This possibility is always open.

Reference Matter

Notes

INTRODUCTION

1. Antonin Artaud, *The Theatre and Its Double*, in *Collected Works*, vol. 4, trans. Victor Corti (London: John Calder, 1999), pp. 1–6. I italicize. From here on all italics are mine unless otherwise indicated.

2. "In the long run, Shakespeare and his followers have instilled a concept of art for art's sake in us, art on the one hand and life on the other, and we might rely on this lazy, ineffective idea as long as life outside held good, but there are too many signs that everything which used to sustain our lives no longer does so and we are all mad, desperate and sick" (ibid., p. 59).

3. "We must know what we want. If we are all prepared for war, the plague, famine and slaughter, we have no need to say so, we have only to go on as we are. To go on behaving as snobs, to flock to hear such and such a singer, to see such and such a wonderful show which never transcends the world of art . . . such and such an exhibition of painting where impressive forms dazzle us here and there, only by chance, and without being truly conscious of the powers they could arouse" (ibid., p. 59).

4. "In the anguished, catastrophic times we live in, we feel an urgent need for theatre that is not overshadowed by events, but arouses

deep echoes within us and predominates over our unsettled period" (ibid., p. 64).

5. "[O]utward events, political conflicts, natural disasters, revolutionary order and wartime chaos, when they occur on a theatre level, are released into the audience's sensitivity with the strength of an epidemic" (ibid., p. 15).

6. In the context of this introduction I do not distinguish between the question of art in general and literature in particular.

7. Obviously, this scene of judgment is not necessarily contemporary, but characterizes a certain relation to art which has been prevalent since one of the founding texts of Western aesthetics, i.e. Plato's *Republic*, with its harsh judgment of the poets and their condemnation to expulsion from the Republic. What I am interested in here are 1) the contemporary resonances of this ancient scene of judgment, and 2) the essential, structural reasons for the recurrent performance of this scene throughout the history of the Western reflection on art.

8. I intentionally blur in these few remarks the distinction between literature and the various possible conceptions *of* literature, since in the explicit and implicit judgments made in relation to literature this distinction is not very clear, and for good reason, since it is hard, if not impossible, to think of literature outside of any "theoretical" conception, in the large sense of the term.

9. It is well known that Artaud wanted "to have done with the judgment of God," that is a judgment by any transcendent authority.

10. It is, I suggest, from the perspective of these issues that the classic problem of a "defense of literature" has to be rethought. For it is a question of whether this rethinking of the status of literature should take the form of a defense, of an attempt to resist the accusations raised against it and of an argument for its innocence. The answer is a complex one. On the one hand, challenging the traditional relation between the discourses and the traditional conception of authority in the name of which literature was accused and judged might seem like defending literature against its accusers. Yet claiming the status of defense to this move would be problematic, since a de-

fense would presuppose that literature needs an external authority in the name of which it could be defended against other authorities in the name of which it was put on trial. We would thus have to prove that it is useful for something, in the service of some higher discourse, such as ethics or politics, which would justify its existence. But if literature is precisely that which problematizes and puts into question this traditional notion of authority and of judgment, and if literature can only be accused by literature itself, then the very traditional structure of defense seems to be eliminated or neutralized. We are thus faced with a strange kind of "defense" that consists in the very neutralization of the traditional structure of defense and scene of judgment. Yet, even saying that we tentatively accept this neutralization, we still have to deal with another interesting dimension of the question of defense. For, we have seen, literature is still in the position of an accused, this time accused by literature itself or by something heard "within" literature itself, and if, in the case of a certain work, would we want to "defend" it against the accusation of literature, the only way to do so would be *to prove* that it is indeed literature. Yet this kind of proof, like any proof, presupposes the notion of stable criteria and thus of certain authorities which can arbitrate these criteria. But if the only "authority" relevant in this case is that of literature itself, there are obviously no possible criteria for a justification of something even as literature. What is thus revealed to us is the *essential nature of literature as accused*. It is accused, and necessarily so, by being a discourse whose authority cannot be guaranteed outside its actual taking place. Its speech is thus orphaned, unable to show or prove its claims to a name and position of its own. Thus, if on the one hand this new positioning of the problem of literature is indeed a "defense" by neutralizing the traditional scene of judgment, then on the other hand and at the same time it exposes literature as essentially, and irrecoverably, accused.

11. "I want to attempt a terrific feminine. The cry of claims, of trampled down rebellion, of steeled anguish at war. The lamentation of an opened abyss, as it were; the wounded earth cries out . . . to

vent this cry I must exhaust myself . . . but I must fall in order to scream this struck-down cry . . . yet the cry I have uttered first invokes a pocket of silence, withdrawn silence. . . . A properly understood rhythm proceeds thus in all true theatre" (ibid., pp. 113–16).

12. "The Theatre of Cruelty was created in order to restore an impassioned convulsive concept of life to theatre" (p. 94).

13. "One of the many things language does for us, however, is to render knowledge a communal possession, or at least a communicable, and so transmissible, property. There is a fluctuating body of knowledge possessed in common by a community, not of course in the sense that all its members are cognizant of everything it comprises, but in the weaker sense that it is in principle accessible to all." Michael Dummett, "Testimony and Memory," in *The Seas of Language* (Oxford: Oxford University Press, 1997), p. 422.

14. It is not a question, of course, of being unable to *know about* the existence of disastrous events such as the French Revolution or the Holocaust. There is historical evidence and documentation that can provide us with knowledge. Rather, it is a matter of what it would mean to relate to these events *as* revolution, or *as* disaster and not simply as knowledge. But it is not only a question of grand historical events; there are events such as falling in love with a person or with a work of art that leave no trace or documentation, and it is not at all clear what it could mean to know about them outside of their actual taking place.

15. See respectively Emmanuel Levinas, *Otherwise Than Being or Beyond Essence* (Dordrecht/Boston/London: Kluwer Academic Publishers, 1991); Jacques Derrida, *Demeure: Fiction and Testimony* (Stanford: Stanford University Press, 2000); Jean-François Lyotard, *The Differend* (Minneapolis: University of Minnesota Press, 1988); Giorgio Agamben, *Remnants of Auschwitz—The Witness and the Archive* (New York: Zone Books, 1999); Shoshana Felman, *Testimony: Crises of Witnessing in Literature, Psychoanalysis, and History* (New York and London: Routledge, 1992).

16. Which does not mean, of course, that there are no facts out-

side of their transmission. But the event as event is nowhere but in its transmission.

17. This definition of the actor as the becoming of an event which s/he witnessed and has to transmit is not necessarily opposed, contrary to a possible first impression, to such celebrated conceptions of the actor as Brecht's or Bresson's. In the case of Brecht, the actor is encouraged to speak as if s/he is quoting the character, speaking in the third person, keeping a distance from it; in the case of Bresson, who opposed the very idea of professional acting, the actor is asked to speak "without" emotion, as if the role is spoken by the words themselves without the personal intervention or interpretation of the actor. What both these conceptions oppose is a certain psychologistic understanding of the actor as someone who becomes or assumes a certain identity with which s/he empathizes. What happens in Brecht as well in Bresson is that a certain foreignness is introduced into the acting itself, as if the actor does not speak, but is spoken by something else which is different from him/her as a psychological personality. It is this foreignness, I suggest, to which the witness precisely testifies. What *speaks through* the witness is the event, which s/he becomes not as an identity of a character, but perhaps as an emotion. Although emotion would now have to be understood differently than it was by Brecht and Bresson, not as psychological, but as the very e-motion, or the movement, of the event through the witness. Becoming actor signifies a being moved to perform.

18. I intentionally conflate in these discussions literature with "theatre" and avoid any distinctions that are usually drawn by theoreticians of drama between the two. The "dramatic" aspects peculiar to theatre do not, I suggest, have to be thought of as some extra dimension beyond the textual dimension of literature. Rather, the point is to rethink all these categories and distinctions which are still metaphysical in an attempt to think a "theatre" or "literature" of the future which announces the dissolution of the traditional, stable categories, distinctions, and definitions of literature and theatre.

19. This is what is essential even in a case like Foucault's where it

is the thought of the political that is often at the center of his reflections on power.

20. Paul De Man, *Aesthetic Ideology* (Minneapolis: University of Minnesota Press, 1996), p. 133. Italics De Man's; boldface mine.

21. Gilles, Deleuze, *Foucault* (Minneapolis: University of Minnesota Press, 1988), p. 74. I italicize.

22. Hannah Arendt, *Qu'est-ce que la Politique?* (Paris: Editions du Seuil, 1995). Translation mine.

23. Ibid., p. 72.

24. Stephen Greenblatt, *Renaissance Self Fashioning* (Chicago: University of Chicago Press, 1980), p. 142.

25. Ibid., p. 145.

26. Ibid., p. 136.

27. Ibid., pp. 142, 143.

28. This thought of the dissolution of context, which I propose announces a new dimension of thinking, occurs in a philosopher like Emmanuel Levinas as the thinking of the Other. He can thus say "the Other comes to us not only out of context but also without mediation," in *Basic Philosophical Writings*, ed. Adriaan T. Peperzak, Simon Critchley, and Robert Bernasconi (Bloomington: Indiana University Press, 1996), p. 53.

29. A crisis famously articulated by sayings such as Nietzsche's that "Europe is sick."

30. D. H. Lawrence, *Studies in Classic American Literature* (London: Penguin Books, 1977), pp. 7, 8.

31. Quoted in Donald Pease, *Visionary Compacts* (Madison: University of Wisconsin Press, 1987), p. 4, and taken from *Studies in Classic American Literature*, although I could not find it in my edition of Lawrence's book.

32. *Studies in Classic American Literature*, p. 14.

33. Thus Cavell, following Emerson, views America as an unprecedented and revolutionary event that in a way is always yet to come: "Why is this new America said to be yet unapproachable? There are many possibilities, three obvious ones. First, it is unap-

proachable if he (or whoever belongs there) is already there (always already), but unable to experience it, hence to know or tell it; or unable to tell it, hence to experience it. Second, finding a nation is not managed by landfall; a nation speaks of birth. There is no nation if it has only one inhabitant. Emerson's sentence speaks of being born again, out of nature and into his discovery; and 'born again' implies that there is (or was) another, one from which to be born. Are two enough? Third, this new America is unapproachable by a process of continuity, if to find it is indeed (to be ready) to be born again, that is to say, suffer conversion; conversion is to be turned around, reversed, and that seems to be a matter of *discontinuity*." Stanley Cavell, "Finding as Founding: Taking Steps in Emerson's 'Experience,'" in *This New Yet Unapproachable America: Lectures After Emerson After Wittgenstein* (Albuquerque: Living Batch Press, 1989), pp. 91–92. Cavell italicizes.

34. It seems to me that Lawrence's conception of classic "American" literature demands that the notorious question of the canon be rethought. The debates about the canon usually take one of two forms—either the very notion of a canon is accused of being in essence an authoritarian and totalitarian one, representing the ideology and voices of those in power, usually white, European, males, and repressing other, weaker, voices; or, the idea of a canon is accepted as valid, yet it is claimed that we simply need to expand it, to give in it representation to more and more voices, like those of women, blacks, non-westerners and others who have not been heard. It seems to me that both attitudes should be problematized in the light of a view of literature as "America" or as that which is in excess of itself and whose authority, as I have suggested above, emanates from itself and can be heard only "within" or as literature. That is, if the conception of the canon indeed depends on a traditional logic of authority and of judgment whereby some "external" discourse to literature arbitrates and judges what is important and what is not, what is central and what is not and so forth, then indeed we might wish to invalidate it as a notion. Yet doing so would still invoke the name of some other author-

ity, some other discourse or power—let us say the legal discourse of rights, in the name of the rights of women, blacks and other marginalized groups—then we still remain caught in the traditional logic of authority, and nothing has changed but a shift in power. The same can be said for the attempts to expand the canon in the name of other voices, an expansion that still adheres to the logic of representation, which is a logic of in-the-name-of, or of authority, and still retains the traditional notion of the canon. But if we understand the canon as always a canon of classic "American" literature then we completely shift ground, for the canon, and the paradigmatic works that comprise it, are now understood as having to do with the birth of an authority as wound, as "America"—but we might also now say as "Women" or as "Blacks"—a wound which is indeed an accusation against literature, and which is in excess of literature, but which can be heard only within or as literature, in certain "canonical" works whose privilege it is to have somehow witnessed and transmitted wounds in an especially powerful way. Thus "women," "blacks," "America," etc. are now names for disastrous events which inflict wounds on something called "white-male-Europe," disasters that put literature into question in the name of an event heard only as literature, and encapsulating a revolutionary promise for a literature yet to come. The canon thus loses its religious and authoritarian origin and becomes a canon-ball, a disastrous/revolutionary weapon exploding into the future.

35. Lawrence's way of reading America (or at least this aspect of it) radically differs from other dominant readings of America from the perspective of the European crisis and collapse. These latter viewed America either as a possible continuation in a new site of the collapsing European project or as a utopia in which sick Europe can find refuge. Thus Michael Hardt and Antonio Negri suggest in a recent book that "The refusal of European consciousness to recognize its decline often took the form of projecting its crisis onto the American utopia. That projection continued for a long time, as long as lasted the necessity and urgency to rediscover a site of freedom that could

continue the teleological vision of which Hegelian historicism is perhaps the highest expression." And also: "In a certain sense, then, it seemed as if the continuity that existed between U.S. history and the history of Europe was broken and that the United States had embarked on a different course, but really the United States represented for these Europeans the resurrection of an idea of freedom that Europe had lost." Michael Hardt and Antonio Negri, *Empire* (Cambridge, Mass.: Harvard University Press, 2000), pp. 383, 381.

36. And we might expand this category to include such "European" writers as Hölderlin, Kleist, Kafka, and Mallarmé.

37. "Hawthorne and His Mosses," in the Norton critical edition of Herman Melville, *Moby-Dick; Or, The Whale*, ed. Harrison Hayford and Hershel Parker (New York and London: W. W. Norton, 1967), p. 546. Obviously, these declarations can be understood as, and probably partially are, expressions of nationalistic chauvinism, yet it seems to me that something much darker and disturbing is at stake in this challenge to Europe and its literature raised here.

38. Nick Selby, ed., *Herman Melville: Moby-Dick—Essays, Articles, Reviews* (New York: Columbia University Press, 1998), p. 8. Selby italicizes.

39. All these kind of references will be usually limited to the notes.

40. Antonin Artaud, *Selected Writings*, ed. Susan Sontag (Berkeley and Los Angeles: University of California Press, 1988), p. 266.

CHAPTER I

1. "The Moses of Michelangelo," in Sigmund Freud, *Writings on Art and Literature* (Stanford: Stanford University Press, 1997), pp. 122, 123.

2. Ibid., p. 123. In the context of this chapter it is not important to decide whether Freud submits himself in his essay to what Lacoue-Labarthe calls a dialectic of the sublime, and thus attempts to transcend this enigmatic moment to which he structurally points. We are only concerned with the structure that Freud reveals and the insight

involved with such a structure, and not the way in which he interprets or responds to it. For a discussion of Freud's movement as being dialectical, see Phillipe Lacoue-Labarthe's "Sublime Truth," in Jefferey S. Librett, ed., *Of the Sublime: Presence in Question* (Albany: SUNY Press, 1993), pp. 86–87.

3. Henceforth all quotations from *Moby-Dick* will be taken from Harrison Hayford, Hershel Parker, and G. Thomas Tanselle, eds.: Herman Melville, *Moby-Dick or The Whale*, Northwestern-Newberry Edition (Evanston, Ill.: Northwestern University Press, 2001). All emphases henceforth, unless otherwise indicated, are mine.

4. Alfred Kazin, "Introduction to *Moby-Dick*," in Richard Chase, ed., *Melville: A Collection of Critical Essays* (Englewood Cliffs, N.J.: Prentice Hall, 1962), p. 39.

5. Donald Pease, "Melville and Cultural Persuasion," in Myra Jehlen, ed., *Herman Melville—A Collection of Critical Essays* (Englewood Cliffs, N.J.: Prentice Hall, 1994), p. 69.

6. Ibid., p. 67.

7. Ibid., p. 69.

8. In the words of Marc Richir: "Il faudra à Melville quarante ans pour retrouver, avec *Billy Budd*, quelque chose de *Moby-Dick*, et dans l'équilibre entre le désenchantement et l'élan visionnaire. Rythme combien lent du *retour de forces* quasi intactes, temperées et mesurées par la lumière de la vieillesse." Marc Richir, *Melville—les assises du monde* (Paris: Hachette, 1998), p. 97. I am not interested in this context in deciding whether this judgment is correct or not, whether the years in which Melville wrote Clarel and turned to poetry be considered years of silence or of decline. What interests me here is simply the fact that critics found it necessary to use the vocabulary of power in a significant manner also when discussing Melville's life.

9. This critical oversight, perhaps even repression, of the importance of the question of power for the Melvillean oeuvre in general and for *Moby-Dick* in particular, characterizes, as far as I know, all of the critical literature on Melville with the notable exception of Gior-

gio Agamben's illuminating discussion of the Aristotelian concepts of power (*dynamis* and *energeia*) in his discussion of Melville's short story *Bartleby the Scrivener* in his "Bartleby, or On Contingency," in *Potentialities—Collected Essays in Philosophy* (Stanford: Stanford University Press, 1999).

CHAPTER 2

1. Or, in the terms of another of Melville's enigmatic novels, is the narrator a man to put your confidence in, or is he a confidence man?

2. For a recent account of the relations between fiction and testimony see Jacques Derrida's *Demeure—Fiction and Testimony*.

3. As I have mentioned in the introduction, the novel's ambiguity was, from the very beginning, a source for both frustration and wonder for its readers. Thus writes Melville's friend Evert Duyckink in his review of *Moby-Dick* from 1851: "A difficulty in the estimate of this, in common with one or two other of Mr. Melville's books, occurs from the *double character under which they present themselves*. In one light they are romantic fictions, in another statements of absolute fact. . . . It becomes quite impossible to submit such books to a distinct classification as fact, fiction, or essay."

4. Ishmael was Abraham's firstborn son conceived with Hagar, his slave; Hagar and Ishmael were sent into exile after the birth of Abraham's second son, Isaac, born of his wife Sarah.

5. There are of course other possibilities implied by this extremely complex structure of address. I simply wanted to show what I take to be its main directions and the textual dynamic that generates its possibilities.

6. Melville meditates on these relations among the questions of the name, of fiction, and of abandonment in the famous and familiar lines from "Hawthorne and His Mosses": "Would that all excellent books were foundlings, without father or mother, that so it might be, we could glorify them without including their ostensible authors. . . . I know not what would be the right name to put on the title page of an

excellent book, but this I feel, that the names of all fine authors are fictitious ones." The Norton critical edition of *Moby-Dick*, ed. Hayford and Parker, p. 536.

7. The Hebrew name Ishmael already incorporates the notion of call or address, since its meaning is God will hear.

8. It will be our task to examine what are the relations between authority and power, for they are not exactly synonymous.

9. The passage quoted above in which Ishmael holds to the truth of his testimony is taken from a chapter entitled "Affidavit," which means, in legal terminology, the giving of a written declaration under oath before a public official.

10. We can thus already see that the name Ishmael cannot serve as a unified source of authority or power, as it does for example in the Pease quotation above, since Ishmael's discourse precisely functions as a site of undecidability and problematizes the notion of authority and linguistic power.

11. Of course, Ishmael's abdication of authority should not be taken merely at face value. The question of when someone, and if someone, abandons authority is a highly complex one. Yet for the moment, it is sufficient to indicate this aspect of Ishmael's relation to authority. Nevertheless, we can already point out that in these opening pages, following his declaration to abdicate authority in favor of the life of a simple sailor, Ishmael's ambivalence toward this abdication is revealed when he says: "True, they rather order me about some. . . . And at first, this sort of thing is unpleasant enough. It touches one's sense of honor, particularly if you come from an old established family in the land. . . . And more than all, if just previous to putting your hand into the tar-pot, *you have been lording it as a country school-master, making the tallest boys stand in awe of you.* The transition is a keen one . . . and requires a strong decoction of Seneca and the Stoics to enable you to grin and bear it. But even this wears off in time" (p. 6).

12. The point that Ahab breaks the law of whaling is made by Gilles Deleuze in his important and visionary essay "Bartleby; or, The

Formula," in *Essays Critical and Clinical* (Minneapolis: University of Minnesota Press, 1997).

13. For example, in the famous chapter "Cetology" which attempts to produce an exhaustive scientific systematization of the whale, Ishmael finally has to concede the failure of his efforts (although somewhat ironically, and only in relation to its scientific status, at this point): "I now leave my cetological system standing thus unfinished, even as the great Cathedral of Cologne was left, with the crane still standing upon the top of the uncompleted tower" (p. 145).

14. It seems to me that the question of the whale and its relation to authority problematizes and calls into question such efforts as Wai-chee Dimock's to raise the question of authority as it pertains to Melville and *Moby-Dick*. In a discussion of Melville's enterprise and its relation to authority, Dimock speaks about "the formal logic by which Melville executes his authorial dictates, supervises and legitimates, affixes meanings and assigns destinies," and she adds, "This textual governance, I believe, cannot be divorced from the social governance of antebellum America, for the terms of Melville's authorial sovereignty, by which he fashions his textual universe into a textual given, are ultimately analogous to the terms of America's national sovereignty, by which the social universe is fashioned into a social given. From this perspective, Melville's authorial practices are neither strictly private nor even strictly literary, for what they adumbrate, in their controlling logic of form, is something like a controlling 'logic of culture.'" *Empire for Liberty* (Princeton, N.J.: Princeton University Press), p. 7. And, resorting to a criticism of "Melville's authoritarian writing" through an analysis of the historical context of the novel, she writes: "If we are to think of authorship as an articulation of the author's selfhood, and if that selfhood is itself a contingent term within a historical process, then literature too must be understood to be contingent. There is no transcendent ground, ultimately, for its formal authority—its assembly of shape and meaning—because the 'author' who authorizes that form is himself historically constituted . . . for the 'text' and its 'context' are in every case inseparable, the lat-

ter being not so much external to the former as constitutive of it, encompassing it and permeating it as the condition of its textuality" (ibid., p. 5). I would argue that Dimock partially ignores the possibility that Melville's novel is itself an extraordinarily complex meditation on the question of authority, its problematization, and its critique. By resorting to the couple of text and context she assigns *Moby-Dick* a horizon of meaning that dictates and fixes the possibility of its understanding, thus performing a gesture which might itself be viewed as authoritarian. Questioning the concept of authority always involves as well a questioning of hermeneutic principles such as reading a text via its context. What the whale offers us and demands of us, I suggest, is a thinking which exceeds the thinking of context as the condition of possibility of that which arrives at its midst, a thinking of that which cannot be grasped and assigned a place in the order established by stable and stabilizing historical/contextual interpretations (see also my discussion of Greenblatt in the introduction). It is thus that the famous section of extracts that precedes *Moby-Dick*'s first chapter is composed of contextless fragments, all of which simply deal with the whale, yet without any knowledge of their historical context. This fragmentary section thus allegorically shows the whale to be essentially related to the question of the contextless fragment.

15. The unstable quality of Ishmael's discourse seems to point again to its strong affinity—with which we opened chapter one—with another scientific-testimonial-fabulous writer, i.e., Sigmund Freud.

16. "'Perhaps' is the modality of an enigma, irreducible to the modalities of being and certainty." Emmanuel Levinas, "Enigma and Phenomenon," in *Basic Philosophical Writings*, p. 67.

17. This unidentifiability of the address of the whale due to its fundamental ambiguity suggests that the position taken in relation to it is close to Heideggerian anxiety. Jean-Luc Marion characterizes this anxiety as follows: "Anxiety does not know who or what threatens; *it does not even know with certitude whether a threat actually threatens or whether it is only a matter of the imagination.*" *Reduction and Given-*

ness—*Investigations of Husserl, Heidegger, and Phenomenology* (Evanston, Ill.: Northwestern University Press, 1998), p. 175, emphasis mine.

18. This logic will not be that of the traditional philosophical concept. Michel Haar, describing the character of Nietzsche's key words (Will to Power, Nihilism, Overman, Eternal Return) characterizes their opposition to traditional philosophical concepts in a way which seems to me particularly relevant to Melville's key word in this text, the whale (and also, as a consequence, the "identities" Ishmael and Ahab). Haar says: "Whereas a concept, in the classical sense, comprises and contains, in an identical and total manner, the content that it assumes, most of Nietzsche's key words bring forth . . . a plurality of meanings undermining any logic based on the principle of identity. Insofar as they include significations that are incompatible with each other, these words might be understood as bursting at the seams." *Nietzsche and Metaphysics* (Albany: SUNY Press, 1996), p. 3. This point of comparison between Nietzsche's enterprise and Melville's is obviously not the only one that can be made about these two great thinkers who are so close to each other in many respects, most notably, the way they place the question of power at the center of their works.

CHAPTER 3

1. Thus the forces of life will never behave in the manner of mechanistic forces, since what governs them is not an economy of calculation, but the surprise of provocation.

2. Ahab himself articulates the sense that it is precisely his body that is the limit to his power, the name of his helplessness: "Oh, oh, oh! how this splinter gores me now! Accursed fate! that the unconquerable captain in the soul should have such a craven mate! 'Sir?' 'My body, man, not thee" (p. 560) and "Ye see an old man cut down to the stump; leaning on a shivered lance; propped up on a lonely foot. 'Tis Ahab—his body's part; but Ahab's soul's a centipede, that moves upon a hundred legs" (p. 561).

3. That is, the bleeding which Ishmael refers to as flowing between the body and the soul, which is thus located between the literal (bodily) and the metaphorical understanding of bleeding (see also discussion in note 5, chapter 3).

4. In this sense, the signifyingness of the whale "behind the mask," as Ahab says, seems to be very close to Levinas's understanding of the signifyingness of the Other: "The proximity of the other is the meaningfulness of the face . . . *signifying directly from beyond the plastic forms that* mask the face by their presence in perception." *Of God Who Comes to Mind* (Stanford: Stanford University Press, 1998), p. 162, emphasis mine.

5. This shocking event of wounding that Ahab suffers can quite obviously be read as a traumatic event in the psychoanalytic sense of the term. Cathy Caruth, in the introduction to her *Unclaimed Experience*, reminds us that the "Greek Trauma, or wound, originally referred to an injury inflicted on the body. In its later usage, particularly in the medical and psychiatric literature, and most centrally in Freud's text, the term trauma is understood as a wound inflicted not upon the body, but upon the mind." But, Caruth adds, "what seems to be suggested by Freud in *Beyond the Pleasure Principle* is that the wound of the mind—the breach in the mind's experience of time, self, and the world—is not, like the wound of the body, a simple and healable event, but rather an event that . . . is experienced too soon, too unexpectedly, to be fully known and is therefore not available to consciousness until it imposes itself again, repeatedly, in the nightmares and repetitive actions of the survivor." *Unclaimed Experience: Trauma, Narrative, and History* (Baltimore: Johns Hopkins University Press, 1996). I mostly subscribe to this description, and to its account, which as we will see operates in Ahab as well, of the repetition of the event as nightmare. What seems to me problematic, though, is the still too metaphysical opposition between what Caruth calls "the simple and healable bodily wound" and the wound of the mind. What is at stake in Ahab's case, I have begun to show, is the inextricable and enigmatic entanglement of what Ishmael calls the body and soul, or what

Caruth calls the body and mind. There is nothing simple about the wound of the body, and understanding the nature of the mind involves us precisely in understanding the nature of the *body as wound*. The metaphorical slippage between the two wounds (to the body and to the soul or mind) is precisely what this whole novel tries to explore, which makes this slippage something else than metaphor, it makes it perhaps the main enigma upon which language is constituted. We might also suggest that this slippage is precisely the origin of time, as the novel understands it, since Ahab's madness does not follow instantaneously from the wound to his body but depends on the delay between his bodily injury and the subsequent wound of the soul. This delay, which is precisely the bleeding, is the opening of time, and we might thus say that time is precisely the bleeding between the two wounds. The difference between Ahab's traumatic wound as the opening of time and a "simple wound" to a living body is exemplified by the novel in an extraordinary scene of wounding, this time not of Ahab but of the living body that is the whale (a whale that is not Moby Dick). "At the instant of the dart an ulcerous jet shot from this cruel wound, and goaded by it into more than sufferable anguish, the whale now spouting thick blood, with swift fury blindly darted at the craft, bespattering them and their glorying crews all over with showers of gore. . . . It was his death stroke. For, by this time, so spent was he by loss of blood, that he helplessly rolled away from the wreck he had made; lay panting on his side, impotently flapped with his stumped fin, then over and over slowly revolved like a waning world; turned up the white secrets of his belly; lay like a log, and died" (p. 358). Like Ahab, the whale suffers a terrible wound from which he bleeds helplessly, and like Ahab he is filled with instant, bodily fury after being wounded; but unlike Ahab he is not filled with mad monomania. The whale simply bleeds to death and never suffers the exposure to time that is the bleeding between the bodily wound and the wound to the soul. The difference, then, between Ahab's traumatic wounding and the whale's is time ("for time began with man"—says Melville, p. 457); this is also the reason why the whale, as a living body, is always a monster "having been before all time" (p. 457). Thus, not only chronologically, but also essentially). Thus, unlike the whale, it seems that Ahab outlives, survives, his bodily bleeding, and instead starts bleeding between body and soul. Time becomes Ahab's manner of bleeding. We might thus say that, like the whale, Ahab bleeds continuously to death, but unlike the whale, his bleeding is prolonged into an entire life. *The human, like the whale, bleeds to death, but human bleeding becomes an entire life-time.*

6. It is crucial to point out here, that while indeed Ahab's wound points to and raises the question of meaning and sense, it is itself not meaningful, not a sign of anything. Ahab indeed wishes to close it as a sign and give it meaning, and thus to spiritualize it, yet from our perspective this is precisely a tyrannical interpretation of the question of sense raised by the sign. The point is not to spiritualize the wound and turn it into meaning.

7. A relation that Ishmael as the proponent of truth denied, in the quotation given above (see p. 37).

8. Walter Benjamin, *The Origin of German Tragic Drama* (London and New York: Verso, 1998), p. 233.

9. The relation between the question of the whale and the question of delivering letters (in both senses of the word), brought up several times in the novel, is established on the very first page, in the first quotation, taken from Hackluyt, in the "Etymology": "While you take in hand to school others, and to teach them by what name a whalefish is to be called in our tongue, leaving out, through ignorance, the *letter H, which almost alone maketh up the signification of the word*, you *deliver* that which is not true" (p. xvii). We might even speculate, somewhat wildly to be sure, that the two characters for whom the encounter with the whale holds the significance of a singular event, i.e. Ishmael and Ahab, are also the two characters with the letter H in their name (although, unfortunately for my theory, Tashtego also has an h) as if this silent letter was branded or tattooed onto their skin as an undecipherable destiny. This theory seems to me all the more persuasive because of God's decree, on the occasion of his covenant with

Abram announcing the birth of Isaac, that Abram will be henceforth called Abra(h)am, adding a Hebrew "heh" (H) to his name, and his Sarai will be called Sara(h). Significantly, this episode follows the episode describing Ishmael's birth. See *Genesis* 17.

10. Or, in another extraordinary formulation of the power of the drive, Ahab cries out: "What is it, what nameless, inscrutable, unearthly thing is it; what cozening, hidden lord and master, and cruel, remorseless emperor commands me; that against all natural lovings and longings, I so keep pushing . . . recklessly making me ready to do what in my own, proper, natural heart, I durst not so much as dare? Is Ahab, Ahab?" (p. 545). The drive thus has to do with an enigmatic exposure to what is "unnatural" and "inhuman," a monstrous exposure.

11. This point is, for example, emphasized by Ahab's temporary collapse toward the end of the book, when he is thrown from the hunting boat and helplessly exposed to the sea's immensity: "[H]elpless Ahab's head was seen, like a tossed bubble *which the least chance shock might burst*. . . . Dragged into Stubb's boat with bloodshot, blinded eyes, the white brine caking in his wrinkles; the long tension of Ahab's bodily strength did crack, and helplessly he yielded to his body's doom" (p. 551).

12. This creation of the drive and of desire on the boundary between the body and meaning, as a new configuration which belongs to neither and which puts into question the metaphysical opposition between body and soul, is very close to the Freudian analysis of the drive, defined by Serge Leclaire thus: "According to his [Freud's] definition the drive should be taken as a 'concept on the frontier between the mental and the somatic' or even, as he adds in the same sentence, 'as the psychical representative of the stimuli originating from within the organism and reaching the mind, as a measure of the demands made upon the mind for work in consequence of its connection with the body.'" *Psychoanalyzing* (Stanford: Stanford University Press, 1998), p. 39. And a bit later on Leclaire adds: "the difficult concept of the drive, which constitutes Freud's true contribution, tends

to comprehend precisely this dualism [between the psychic and the organic] within a truly novel dynamism. The originality of this concept, described as a limit, is that it grounds the unconscious outside the categories of the biological and the psychological understood in their pre-Freudian senses. In other words, the division or gap grounding the dimension of representation in the whole doctrine of the drives is without question situated elsewhere and otherwise than in the traditional opposition between the soul and the body" (ibid., p. 40).

13. And Ahab, not only through his name (which is of course that of a famous Biblical ruler) is often designated as a powerful king: "Oh, he [Ahab] ain't Captain Bildad; no, and he ain't Captain Peleg; *he's Ahab*, boy; and Ahab of old, thou knowest, was a crowned king!" (p. 79, Melville italicizes) or, "How could one look at Ahab then, seated on that tripod of bones, without bethinking him of the royalty it symbolized? For a Khan of the plank, and a king of the sea, and a great lord of Leviathans was Ahab" (p. 129). A king, by definition we might say, is the lord and king of the Leviathan (an obvious allusion to Hobbes) while the whale is, precisely, the revolutionary principle that wounds this lord of the Leviathan, and undermines his/her authority.

14. The absolute, by definition, is that which does not enter into any relation with a known quality from experience, which is unconditioned and cannot be reduced to any causal explanations. It always has to do with an event that is unpredictable and surprising and that overwhelms the subject.

15. I would suggest that the book that is *Moby-Dick*, dedicated and addressed to Hawthorne, that is, to the author of *The Scarlet Letter* (and it is the only dedication in the Melvillean corpus), can itself be viewed as "responding in kind" (to use an expression of Stanley Cavell) to Hawthorne's cry with Melville's wail, or exposing his singular wound to Hawthorne's singular wound, thus constituting the relations between the two books and the two writers as an exchange of letters. (Hawthorne and Melville were indeed corresponding with

each other at the time of the writing of *Moby-Dick*). Indeed, I would suggest that a certain vision of literary history is implied in this exchange of cries, a non-Bloomian vision of literary history, which is not structured as an Oedipal scene with the anxiety of influence inscribed in it, but rather as a history where the past calls out as a wound or a cry that can only be heard and transmitted to the future through a response in kind, through an additional wail. Thus, speaking about the whale, and we could now say "wail," Ishmael says: "In life, the visible surface of the Sperm Whale is not the least among the many marvels he presents. Almost invariably it is all over obliquely crossed and recrossed with numberless straight marks in thick array, something like those in the finest Italian line engravings. But these marks do not seem to be impressed upon the isinglass substance above mentioned, but seem to be seen through it, as if they were *engraved upon the body itself*. . . . [t]hese are hieroglyphical" (p. 306) Thus the whale (wail) has to do with marvelous (and wounding) signifying scars, or enigmatic marks upon the body.

16. The *Oxford English Dictionary* gives the definition of this verb as "to mark the flesh." An additional definition is "to choose, to select." Thus understanding language through the verb "to wale" means that the cry as a transmitted signifying scar has the character of a bodily laceration which is at the same time a singular election. To be chosen, as Ahab is by the whale, and as the sailors are by Ahab, is to be marked in the flesh with an enigmatic signature (hence the relation between the Jewish conception of the chosen people and the circumcision, and the Christian understanding of saints chosen to suffer the stigmata). In relation to these meditations we can see how Ahab's scar is a striking reinterpretation of Odysseus' scar (which takes it in the direction of the mark of Cain). If *Moby-Dick* can also be said to be a reinterpretation of *The Odyssey* (Maurice Blanchot, for example, in his essay "The Siren's Song," attempts to think these two works together), then at its core this reinterpretation might be said to involve a new interpretation of the scar. If, in Odysseus' case, the scar, as an identity mark, is that which allows for a return home from weary travels at sea,

for a reestablishment of a stable identity and the reoccupation of land and the position of the father, then, in Ahab's case, the scar means precisely the opposite. For Ahab the scar means the shattering of the "I" which was a master in its home, an abandonment by the father or the father function, and the loss of the stability of land and exposure to the forceful winds of the sea. Thus, paradoxically, being chosen or being marked means precisely being dispossessed and exiled.

17. The question is: whether there is another form of desire, one that is associated with the destabilizing principle of the cry, or whether desire, by definition, is the desire of the tyrant. In any case, desire will be used here in the sense of the tyrannical and possessive desire for mastery.

18. This analysis is indebted to two highly interesting and useful texts: Serge Leclaire's intriguing chapter "Taking the Body Literally, or How to Speak of the Body," in his book *Psychoanalyzing*, and Alphonso Lingis's illuminating chapter on Levinas's phenomenology of the face, "Face to Face," in *Deathbound Subjectivity* (Bloomington: Indiana University Press, 1989).

19. I deliberately maintain a certain ambiguity, since it seems to me inevitable, in understanding the enigma that is the whale. On the one hand, the address of the whale can be seen as an allegory of the very constitution of the human body as one governed by relations among sense, sensation, and sensuality, thus as the very constitution of the conditions of possibility of language, the physical senses, and sexual desire. On the other hand, the whale is an event in the history of the already constituted subject, which in a way is only a theoretical fiction, both revealing the constitution established by what we may call the primal whale/wail and constituting the subject anew by assigning it a new destiny and orientation, a new call for language, and a new form of desire.

20. For it is "jealousy presiding over all creations" (p. 164).

21. Stanley Cavell, in a remarkable essay on *Othello* ("Othello and the Stake of the Other," in *Disowning Knowledge: In Six Plays of Shakespeare* [Cambridge and New York: Cambridge University Press,

1987]) which is highly relevant to this side of Ahab's desirous adventure, has noticed the presence of hell and the demon in the names of the two protagonists, dark Othello and the white Desdemona. We may add that *Des*demona's name also alludes to desire, and thus points to the relation between desire and the demonic which is at the center of Ahab's relation to the whale.

22. Or perhaps we should say more accurately that Ahab's hunt consists of two components: on the one hand there is the teleological aim to destroy the whale and become the master of one's own passivity. On the other hand there is the actual *movement* of the hunt itself in which Ahab, after being exposed to the address of the whale and losing his stability in meaning, has lost his identity and even human shape ("Is Ahab, Ahab? Is it I, God, or who, that lifts this arm?" p. 545) and furiously moves in a realm prior to this or that meaning, prior to this or that identity, where it is no longer clear who is chasing whom, who is Ahab and who is Moby Dick. Perhaps this is what Gilles Deleuze means when he enigmatically describes Ahab's adventure as a *becoming* whale: "Ahab does not imitate the whale, he becomes Moby Dick, he enters into the zone of proximity where he can no longer be distinguished from Moby Dick, and strikes himself in striking the whale" (*Essays Critical and Clinical*, p. 78). This double view of the hunt would correspond to our distinction between the two languages of Ahab as the language of terror and the language of the cry or the wail. On the one hand, Ahab's language strives to reach the point where it is completely in mastery of meaning, where it has overcome the passivity of the body; but, on the other hand, what is actually heard in Ahab's language, beyond what he wishes for, is the very wound of language and its opening in a passivity, which involves this loss of identity of the words, where language is *becoming* an almost inarticulate wail.

23. Melville takes up the story of Babel most explicitly in his short story "The Bell Tower," with its Ahabian hero Banadona (i.e. the one assigned to be abandoned, or more precisely, the one refusing his abandonment, putting a ban on his abandonment) whose fate, like

Ahab's, culminates in his being consumed by the mechanical drive that controls him, for he is killed by a clock which he himself has constructed.

24. This reduction into one is what Hannah Arendt calls total domination in her study of totalitarianism, and according to her it always characterizes the effort of totalitarian regimes: "Total domination, which strives to organize the infinite plurality and differentiation of human beings as if all humanity were just one individual, is possible only if each and every person can be reduced to a never-changing identity of reactions, so that each of these bundles of reactions can be exchanged at random for any other." *Totalitarianism*, part 3 of *The Origin of Totalitarianism* (New York: Harcourt Brace & Co., 1976), p. 136. This reduction into one is also what characterizes, essentially, the drive as a principle of unification: "Inasmuch as drive primordially unifies, it must already anticipate every possible multiplicity, must be able to deal with every multiplicity in its possibility. That is, drive must have already surpassed and overcome multiplicity." Martin Heidegger, *The Metaphysical Foundations of Logic* (Bloomington and Indianapolis: Indiana University Press, 1992), p. 91.

25. In his famous analysis of the psychology of crowds in *Group Psychology and the Analysis of the Ego* (ed. James Strachey [New York: W. W. Norton, 1975]), Freud examines the mechanism of identification with the father figure as standing at the source of the strange power which leaders exercise upon groups and of the emotional tie which group members share with each other. It seems to me that what is suggested by the analysis of the wail and of the infliction with a drive that stands at the source of Ahab's control of the sailors is a moment prior to identification. The cry, or the wail, seems to come before the recognition of a stable figure with which to identify. What is more, we have seen that the cry involves precisely the loss of any stability of figures and identities. It seems as though identification already belongs to the fetishistic moment that follows the penetration by the wail and which attempts to stabilize it and give it a shape. Before the identification with the father, and before the father function,

there was a wounding by the call or the wail, before identity there was an anonymous scar.

26. Shoshana Felman, *Writing and Madness: Literature, Philosophy, Psychoanalysis* (Ithaca: Cornell University Press, 1985), p. 71.

27. Ibid., p. 195.

28. There are several hints in the novel that Ahab always dreams the same dream, the dream of hunting Moby Dick.

29. There is another major figure for the dreamer in the novel, which I will not get to discuss at length, and this is that of the abandoned children, the Ishmaels. This is the other side of the dream of the hunter. The abandoned child is also one who has lost the stability of the land as the stability of the father, or of the father function, a world-shattering wound that is responded to by a dreamy voyage the function of which is to regain this lost stability. The dreamy eyed Telemachus, going in search of his lost father Odysseus, is the major literary reference for this kind of dream, and it shows us again the close relation between *Moby-Dick* and *The Odyssey*.

30. In giving us another glimpse at Ahab's recurring dream in another passage, Ishmael writes: "'Stern all! Oh Moby Dick, I clutch thy heart at last!' Such were the sounds that now came hurtling from out the old man's tormented sleep, as if Starbuck's voice had caused the long dumb dream to speak" (p. 515).

31. In fact, the whale is thus revealed as that which destroys the opposition of without and within and shows their constitution to have been determined by the language of the master.

32. Thus, after magnetizing the crew with his drive and desire in the quarter-deck scene, there still remains an almost unheard element of resistance, which Ahab in his joy ignores: "'God keep me!—keep us all!' murmured Starbuck, lowly. But in his joy at the enchanted, tacit acquiescence of the mate, Ahab did not hear his foreboding invocation. . . . For again Starbuck's eyes lighted up with the stubbornness of life" (pp. 164–65). In another passage Ishmael, relating a dream of a somewhat different nature (since Ishmael is a different kind of dreamer) also connects the discovery of life to the interruption of a

dream and to the discovery of the whale: "It was my turn to stand at the foremast-head; and with my shoulders leaning against the slackened royal shrouds, to and fro I idly swayed in what seemed an enchanted air . . . in that dreamy mood losing all consciousness, at last my soul went out of my body . . . [s]uddenly bubbles seemed bursting beneath my closed eyes; like vices my hands grasped the shrouds; some invisible, gracious agency preserved me; *with a shock I came back to life*. And lo! Close under our lee, not forty fathoms off, a gigantic Sperm Whale lay rolling in the water . . ." (pp. 282–83). This shocking return to life is indeed brought up in the context of, and in relation to, the first murderous chapter in the book, chapter 61, "Stubb Kills a Whale."

33. Jacques Derrida, in an interview with which this book shares a close affinity, says: "The 'thou shall not kill'—with all its consequences, which are limitless—has never been understood within the Judeo-Christian tradition, nor apparently by Levinas, as a 'thou shall not put to death the living in general'. It has become meaningful in religious cultures for which carnivorous sacrifice is essential, as being-flesh. The other, such as this can be thought according to the imperative of ethical transcendence, is indeed the other man: man as other, the other as man" (thus not the other as a living whale/wail). "'Eating Well,' or the Calculation of the Subject: An Interview with Jacques Derrida," in Eduardo Cadava, Peter Connor, and Jean-Luc Nancy, eds., *Who Comes After the Subject?* (New York: Routledge, 1991), p. 113.

34. Thomas Pepper, in a passage which resonates with our attempts here, has noticed that three of Freud's key dreams (The Dream of Irma's Injection, the Wolfman's Dream, and the Dream of the Burning Child) are "about singing, shrieking, screaming, about the relations between silence and screaming"; and he continues: "The surgence of the real [i.e. the Lacanian term, more or less, for what is articulated in this chapter as the enigmatic and surprising event of encounter] in each dream (the formula of trimethylamine, the scream of the Wolfman, the dead child who speaks to his father, and says 'Father, don't you see I'm burning?') all these occurrences *call out of*

their contexts the way a text calls out to be read." *Singularities: Extremes of Theory in the Twentieth Century* (Cambridge and New York: Cambridge University Press, 1997), p. 10.

35. In discussing the question of the hunt, and by relating it to Ahab's desire, I have omitted, due to lack of space, a longer discussion of the hunt, which would consider the sailors' relation to it. I would now like to briefly discuss the relation between Ahab's hunt and the sailors' hunt. The general hunt of the sailors is an economic affair dedicated to exchanging the living body of the whale—*of any whale whatsoever*—for an illumination, that is, according to a major metaphorical motif of the novel, for clarity and meaning: an illumination which can be achieved only through murdering the whale, and burning the oil made from his body: "[T]he whaleman, as he seeks the food of light, so he lives in light. He makes his berth an Aladdin's lamp, and lays him down in it; so that in the pitchiest night, the ship's black hull still houses an illumination. . . . He goes and hunts for oil, so as to be sure of its freshness and genuineness, even as the traveller on the prairie hunts up his own supper of game" (p. 426). In a different articulation, Ishmael writes that a dying hunted whale "[f]or all his old age, and his one arm, and his blind eyes . . . must die the death and be murdered, in order to light the gay bridals and other merry-making of men, and also to illuminate the solemn churches that preach unconditional inoffensiveness by all to all" (p. 357). The affair of hunting is thus, in the general case of the sailors as well, a murderous affair related to a hermeneutic imperative, to bring home, from the unstable and dark sea, clear and stable meaning. It is based on the terroristic principle *par excellence*, to *turn blood into light, into enlightenment*. Yet the difference between this hunt and Ahab's is the following: if Ahab's hunt is an affair of desire, the sailors' hunt is an affair of law. The sailors do not strive after the whale in a manner that indicates that their own destiny and meaning is at stake, but rather simply as an economic affair dictated by a law they do not question, and by a principle of exchange whose meaning and drive remain covered up. Ahab's hunt insists on a *singularity* of desire (even though murderous) and does not

accept any whale whatsoever to satisfy his hunger, any substitution, but only Moby Dick. He thus reveals a dimension prior to economic exchange, a non-economic relation to the excess which is the address of the whale, and which the later, economic one, tries to stabilize and efface: "Though, in overseeing the pursuit of this whale, [not Moby Dick] Captain Ahab had evinced his customary activity, to call it so; yet now that the creature was dead, some vague dissatisfaction, or impatience, or despair, seemed working in him; as if the sight of that dead body reminded him that Moby Dick was yet to be slain; and though a thousand other whales were brought to his ship, all that would not one jot advance his grand, monomaniac object" (pp. 291–92). Ahab's force and domination of the sailors derive partly from the fact that he uncovers the desirous and murderous element, which involves the need to efface the passivity and helplessness of the living body, under the supposedly impersonal law of hunting. A second major difference between Ahab and the sailors, dependent on the first one, is that Ahab's chase after the whale involves an element which is perhaps not murderous and is perhaps beyond the drive, and this is the element of movement and loss of identity involved in the hunt, the becoming-whale, to use Deleuze's expression, or the becoming-wail of his language. In contrast, the sailors' hunt involves no real movement and can be said to be conducted on land, as it were, because they remain within the stability and identity that belongs to the land.

CHAPTER 4

1. And we may note that the appalling contains within it an allusion to whiteness, or to paleness.

2. What seems to me again striking is the similarity between this very complex rhetorical position of Ishmael in relation to the enigma of the whale and Freud's position in relation to the enigma of the unconscious. Freud himself can be said to be a character experiencing the unconscious, a writer dedicating himself to the enigma of the unconscious, and a fabulist/witness trying to persuade of/witness the existence of the unconscious. The same can be said of Heidegger in rela-

tion to the overwhelming enigma of Being, although his rhetorical position seems less complex.

3. The sentence ends on a note of horror and panic, since this is what the sentence's trajectory in its inability to stop discovered; thus the horror that ends the sentence is a reflection of the sentence's own attempts and its failure.

4. The following reflections and remarks about the question of the "who," which is an important issue in this chapter, are indebted to several thinkers. First of all, to Heidegger's famous distinction between the question "what is" which can be applied to things in the natural world, and the question "who is" which is the one proper to the human, a distinction later expanded upon and modified in various ways by Hannah Arendt, Jacques Derrida, Gilles Deleuze, and others. I suggest that *Moby-Dick* defines the human as the one who is addressed by a white and monstrous riddle.

5. The essential gap between the event that is addressed to me, and the as yet unsaid response to the "as who," constitutes the very *rhythm* of any investigation of the very special kind to which this chapter is dedicated.

6. Obviously, I could have put this sentence in a completely different tone, as I did with the retelling of the framing device of the novel, and discussed, for example, the fabulist Ishmael, faking speechlessness and horror, playing the accused martyr, precisely in order to persuade his listeners, manipulated into compassion, of the veracity of his completely implausible "white lie." I will not always be able to raise these other possibilities, although I will at times, but the text should always be read with an ear for them. If I choose to sustain this tonality rather than that one, it is, perhaps, out of personal predilection or attunement, depending on the mood a certain passage inspires me with, and for reasons of economy; yet all these qualifications have little relevance for the polyphonic intention of the argument. The essential point is that whiteness will be precisely the enigma that makes possible and even necessary these inevitable ambiguities, as we will later see more clearly.

7. As we recall, this passage is taken from Ahab's dream quoted above, and describes Ahab's blank or white cry, uttered in his dreams and shattering their attempts at stability. What I am trying to suggest by thus juxtaposing Ahab's white cry and Ishmael's discovery of the white riddle (a suggestion strongly supported by the vocabulary that Ishmael uses, as we will soon see) is that Ishmael's discovery of himself as a white riddle has to be understood as having to do with his exposure to, and, simultaneously, as a reverberation of, Ahab's white cry, to which his investigation (which also takes up the questions of who he is and the enigma of whiteness in general) thus testifies beyond any conscious and knowledgeable scientific or juridical type of testimony. The testimony involved in whiteness is essentially a reverberating testimony, speaking through the witness, sometimes completely unknown to him/her, as an enigmatic white cry addressed to him/her and constituting simultaneously the enigma of who he/she is. Later on in this chapter on whiteness, Ishmael indeed describes whiteness in terms very similar to those of Ahab's cry: "the great principle of light, for ever remains white or colorless in itself, and if operating without medium upon matter, would touch all objects, even tulips and roses with its own black tinge" (p. 195). We might thus say that writing about whiteness is also testifying to Ahab's cry, and that writing about Ahab's cry is a testimony to the discovery of the principle of whiteness. For a theory of the witness, with which these suggestions resonate, as having to do, precisely, with the collapse of the legal, knowing witness and testifying to an unsayable event, see Shoshana Felman's remarkable and moving essay "A Ghost in the House of Justice: Death and the Language of the Law," in *The Juridical Unconscious: Trials and Traumas in the Twentieth Century* (Cambridge, Mass.: Harvard University Press, 2002).

8. I am not saying evil, since evil, in the vocabulary of the novel, occupies precisely the place of whiteness, evil is in a way itself beyond good and bad.

9. Phillipe Jaworski, in an excellent essay from which I have learned much, in his *Melville Le Desert et L'Empire* (Paris: Editions rue d'ulm,

1985), tries to isolate in *Moby-Dick* two types of relation to meaning. The first he calls empire, assigned to Ahab and regarded as a narcissistic and appropriating relation to meaning; and the other he calls nomadic writing, or the language of the desert, which he attributes to Ishmael, and which he sees as an anti-imperial and non-narcissistic language. As close as I am to some of his concerns, it seems to me that this division is still too simplistic. What I have tried precisely to show is that both Ishmael and Ahab are structured upon an internal difference between, to use Jaworski's terms for the moment although their logic is not precisely mine, the language of the empire and the language of the desert, and that this opposition cannot simply be divided between the protagonists, nor is it that simple to overcome. The whale, in the novel, reveals this internal division and mandates the thinking of a new logic of these divisions. This too simplistic opposition between Ishmael and Ahab, given in somewhat similar terms to Jaworski's, can be found in William Spanos, *The Errant Art of Moby-Dick: The Canon, the Cold War, and the Struggle for American Studies* (Durham and London: Duke University Press, 1995). In a way, this opposition is simply a continuation of what Donald Pease and other New Americanists have characterized as the Cold War tradition of Melville interpretation, mentioned above, which saw Ishmael as the pure principle of resistance against Ahab's no less pure oppressive totalitarian power. In general we might say that the either-or Ahab/Ishmael has characterized most of the critical tradition of reading *Moby-Dick*. Thus, while in the earlier phases of *Moby-Dick* criticism the critical attention was mainly paid to the figure of Ahab, in later generations the figure of Ishmael came to the fore as an opposition to Ahab. What I am trying to show in this study is the essential implication of the two and the complex logic that this implication calls for.

10. I am introducing the question of freedom here since it is precisely the main axis along which the tradition of postwar critics tried to read Ishmael's relation to Ahab. And although I agree with these critics that indeed it is the question of freedom which is called for in this context, the logic of this freedom, I will try to show, is much more complex than the opposition of the free Ishmael to the tyrannical Ahab.

11. I have switched in these discussions to the first person, since the adventure of whiteness always has to do with the first person, and more accurately with a "me."

12. We can therefore see another possible function of the famous opening "Call me Ishmael" as a response to which the surprised reader, before any understanding of what is going on, finds him/herself having to ask "who, me?"

13. Thus, if we think of our reading of the book as a white event, we might say that an undecidable question would be "who reads?" — for it is not clear whether it is a "me" reading the book or whether it is the book reading the "me" and reading itself through a "me."

14. "And I only am escaped alone to tell thee": Ishmael quotes from the book of Job at the final page of the book (p. 573).

15. There are obviously also other kinds of events, which everyone can share, yet the special kind of event we are dealing with here, the enigmatic white event (which is, in a way, exactly the same event as any other, yet apprehended in a completely different, white, manner), is that which is structurally revealed only by happening to someone in their singularity. This is not to say, for example, that many people cannot be witnesses to a terrible disaster or to an extraordinary festivity that becomes for all of them a white event—yet even in these cases, the logic of this whiteness demands that for each of them the event will be experienced as a singularizing encounter, having to do with who they are, and thus, in a way, none of them can be said to have experienced the "same" event. Moby Dick, for example, is not the same for Ahab and for Ishmael, because its encounter is a singularizing encounter and thus different for both of them.

16. See introduction for my comments on the actor.

17. For example, testimony about an encounter which caused one to fall in love, or about an overwhelming experience of a work of art, always carries with it, and essentially so, a suspicion of deceit, even of self-deceit, and perhaps even of delusion. As a psychoanalytic aside, of the sort I've been raising every so often, I would like to suggest that this constitutive shadow of delusion haunts, for example, Freud, the

discoverer of, and witness to, the enigmatic unconscious; a shadow of suspicion that leads him to suspect his similarity to the delusional judge Schreber. And he has no authority by himself, as hard as he tries, to overcome this suspicion. Only through a reverberation of and a witnessing to his event of discovery, a witnessing that also has to be an act of freedom on the part of the witness, can this shadow of delusion turn into something else. It seems to me that Jacques Lacan takes on such an enterprise in his third Seminar, which is a reading of Schreber and of Freud's own reading of Schreber, as well as an act of witnessing and a reverberation of Freud's discovery, an attempt to mark his difference from Schreber; and is at the same time an act that frees Lacan from Freud's desire, initiates a white separation from Freud (I suggest that this complex procedure is what "the return to Freud" means). In this sense, Lacan would wish to situate himself in relation to Freud the way that Ishmael is situated in relation to Ahab, while the rest of Freud's inheritors would be like the sailors, completely consumed by Freud's desire, thus in a sense betraying his legacy. It seems to me that this essential structure of reverberation of, a witnessing to, and a freeing white act of separation from, can also characterize Jacques Derrida's project in relation to Heidegger's raising anew, or even his discovering anew, of the enigmatic question of Being (and I suggest that this complex procedure is also what "deconstruction" at its heart means). I would argue that a true act of Reading, that is, reading in its most profound sense, always answers to this structure.

18. Like Ishmael the "I" can offer no external proof of the existence of this whiteness, but at best can insist on its proofless existence: "Though neither knows where lie the nameless things of which the mystic sign gives forth such hints; yet with me ... somewhere those things must exist" (pp. 194–95).

19. That is, even self-proclaimed fabulists and storytellers of imaginary monstrosities can never be sure that what resonates through their speech is not in fact a testimony to a revolutionary and monstrous disaster that speaks through them, unbeknownst to them.

20. With these four points it becomes clear how the logic of whiteness constitutes the relations between the various positions from which Ishmael speaks—see p. 67.

21. We might say that the prophet Jonah, who plays such an important metaphorical role in the novel, is the model for the one chosen despite himself, and whaled into being a prophet, letting that which makes him helpless speak through him.

22. In fact, even this is not completely accurate, since already by being called into a "me," by being a "me," I have already responded, before I have any choice in the matter.

23. For this is precisely what nudity means; it means the discovery of the exposure to other bodies as an event in which who I am is at stake.

24. I am thinking here of Descartes's famous fiction of the evil genius, which more correctly should be understood as the evil genius that is the very opening of fiction. We have already seen the relation between the address of the whale and the question of evil, and we are now in a better position to understand more precisely the function of evil or of the devil as precisely having to do with the opening of this realm before a decision about existence can be made and which for Descartes was that which allowed for the skeptical experiment and which was also the locus of madness. The whale, for the novel, is precisely Melville's equivalent to Descartes's evil genius; and Melville has famously said that the secret formula of the novel is "I baptize you in the name of the devil," that is, I baptize you not in the name of the establishing authority of meaning which is the father, but in the name of that which interrupts such authority, the diabolical whale or wail which opens the realm prior to truth or falsity.

25. See introduction for the way I attempt to position the problem that literature constitutes for our times.

26. And it is precisely this enigma called language that makes of the human essentially a sailor, that is a creature exposed to forces, which he/she tries to classify and in relation to which he/she tries to direct him/herself, and to which they attempt to give directions.

27. As has been shown, for example, by Samuel Otter in *Melville's Anatomies* (Berkeley: University of California Press, 1999).

28. It would be interesting in this context to mention *Moby-Dick's* direct significance to an important twentieth-century literary project written under the sign of the historical disaster of the holocaust: that of the French writer Georges Perec. Perec's major literary preoccupation is a constant attempt to find means to relate to a certain horrible event that cannot be witnessed directly by a knowledgeable and conscious subject, master of his memory, but calls for a different kind of witness, a literary witness, to something that is immemorial in the event but nevertheless addresses the subject. It is thus perhaps not surprising that *Moby-Dick* in particular and Melville in general became one of Perec's major literary reference points, occupying a highly strategic place in several of Perec's works. I would like to take a very brief look at the way that *Moby-Dick* can be said to function within the body of what is arguably Perec's most important and innovative attempt to come to terms with this unique problem of witnessing, his book *W, ou, le souvenir d'enfance*. The book alternates between two or perhaps three narratives, the one an autobiographical, referential narrative, telling rather matter-of-factly Perec's childhood experiences in occupied France during the Second World War, the second, or second and third narratives, telling of some fabulous and imaginary adventures of looking for survivors of a shipwreck, and describing a strange faraway island where the entire life of its inhabitants revolves around a fascistic cult of sports. The main enigma of the text is the nature of the relations between these two narratives—the referential and the fabulous—for they are not presented to us as standing in any hierarchical or causal relations. Already this dual nature of the narrative suggests an affinity between Perec's experience of literature and Melville's, as I have been trying to describe it. It is therefore perhaps no surprise to discover that the book opens under the sign of the problem of witnessing, very similar to the way it is presented in *Moby-Dick*, and that indeed in the very early paragraphs of the book the narrator invokes Ishmael and the problem of whiteness—and it is

practically the only literary work referred to in the book—as the model for his enterprise. The book thus opens in the following way, starting with the fabulous narrative but nevertheless speaking for the whole book (given here in David Bellos's translation): "For years I put off telling the tale of my voyage to W. Today, impelled by a commanding necessity and convinced that the events to which I was witness must be revealed and brought to light, I resolve to defer it no longer. . . . For years I sought out traces of my history, looking up maps and directories and piles of archives. I found nothing, and it sometimes seemed as though I had dreamt, that there had been only an unforgettable nightmare. . . . Whatever may happen now, whatever I may now do, I was the sole depository, the only living memory, the only vestige of that world. That, more than any other consideration, was what made me decide to write . . . I visited this sunken world and this is what I saw there. I am not possessed with the boiling fury of Ahab, but with Ishmael's white reverie, with the patience of Bartleby. Once again, as for so many before me, these latter shall be my guiding spirits." Georges Perec, *W, or, The Memory of Childhood*, trans. David Bellos (Boston, Mass.: David R. Godine, 1988), pp. 3–4. It is not my intention here to perform a reading of this rich book, but only to point to the double manner in which *Moby-Dick* functions in the body of Perec's text, which is indeed the double way that it relates to the problem of literary history as I am trying to sketch it. That is: 1) *Moby-Dick*'s striking duality can be said to provide the conceptual and stylistic model for Perec's attempt at coming to terms with a problem of witnessing to an enigmatic, white event, to which he is the sole witness, through his use of the double narrative structure (a use which cannot be taken completely at face value, for the referential and the fabulous cannot be so easily separated, and they constantly penetrate each other in this text breaking the borders of their supposedly clear distinction); 2) *Moby-Dick* is evoked as a singular literary witness, and this in a double manner. Its singular act of witnessing, by coming before Perec's book and by addressing it, allows Perec in turn to witness, in a sense creating or calling into being his literary performative

Notes to Chapter 4

capacity for witnessing. But in an even more complex manner, *Moby-Dick*'s singular and unheard-of witnessing, being marked and thus wounded by Perec, echoes Perec's witnessing, reverberating it, thus witnessing it in its own turn and introducing Perec into literary history, showing again how it is also the past which has to witness the future. No less than Perec becoming a witness to *Moby-Dick* does *Moby-Dick* become a witness to Perec.

29. See my discussion in the introduction of the literary declaration of independence from European literature that Melville calls for at the time of writing *Moby-Dick* in his essay "Hawthorne and His Mosses."

30. For we remember that Melville has said that the book is written in the name of the devil.

31. Indeed, it can be shown how Melville, in an extremely rigorous and methodical way, turns each chapter into a sort of laboratory, investigating and experimenting with a certain aspect of a single problem which, I argue, is that of the enigmatic address of the whale.

32. See Rudolph Gasche's essay "The Scene of Writing: A Deferred Outset," in *Glyph: Johns Hopkins Textual Studies* 1 (1977), pp. 150–71.

33. Could it be that this failure, this collapse of any authoritative grasp, will be the true act of bearing witness to the whale's life?

34. The analogies to psychoanalysis cry out.

35. Again, an allusion to Babel, which I have shown is always a metaphor for the attempt to grasp or hunt the whale, that which undermines the human mastery of language.

36. Paradoxical in the sense that monstrous here refers to the very aesthetic failure to represent the monster that is the whale.

37. As he previously criticized all scientists.

38. Remember that I previously argued that there is an essential suspicion of delusion in any witnessing of the event of the whale/wail.

39. Unfortunately I am unable in this context to delve into all the marvelous ironies and paradoxes involved in this chapter, but I would like to mention here that those whale pictures criticized by Ishmael as

fabulous and not true to the actual whale in fact represent scenes from fabulous origins and do not claim to be representing the whale at all. These are dragons and all sorts of other mythical monsters which Ishmael decides are actually whales and then criticizes them for being badly represented.

40. Again, the marvelous ambiguity between the singular event of encounter with the whale and its potentially disastrous nature, and the authoritarian nature of the narrator dissuading the reader from checking up on him. Virtually every line in these whale chapters is fraught with all these ambiguities, which I try in vain to articulate a bit here and there. My reading is thus a mere sampling of the logic, but it does not exhaust even a single line with which it deals.

41. And not even by a "me" since one can never really know what it looks like, that is, one can never really be sure about oneself that the whale was indeed witnessed, the whale is always in excess, also over a "me."

42. "But how can I hope to explain myself here; and yet, in some dim, random way, explain myself I must, else all these chapters might be naught" (p. 163).

43. A legal term, which, as I have mentioned before, means the giving of a written declaration under oath before a public official.

44. That is, we have to accept his own authority that the other authorities (as fabulous and monstrous as they sound) are indeed authoritative (authorities, which in their turn, authorize the authority of his own testimony), while previously we had to accept his authority that only his authority is authoritative while others are fabulous and monstrous.

45. This procedure, in which a supposedly scientific and referential argument suddenly slips into an "argument" based on fabulous mythologies without registering a change in the narrator's attitude, is one Ishmael frequently employs; it recurs quite often as a major argumentative technique. It signals, on the one hand, that any means available to get his points across and to persuade are considered acceptable by the rhetorician, and, on the other hand, that the realm of

the fabulous precisely opens, and inevitably so, in the discourse on the whale. There are other possibilities to interpret this slip between the historical and the fabulous, as we will soon see.

46. "Now small fowls flew screaming over the yet yawning gulf; a sullen *white* surf beat against its steep sides; then all collapsed, and the great shroud of the sea rolled on as it rolled five thousand years ago" (p. 572). But for the epilogue of the survivor these are the last words in the novel.

47. And we might add, not even the witness him/herself can bear witness for the witness.

48. Obviously, all our discussions here, when I say that there is only one witness to the disaster, are not dealing with the status of the "facts" of any disaster, but are thinking about the disaster first and foremost in regard to its status as a white event. As such, it is not the "facts" which are at issue but a witnessing to the disaster as a white wail happening to a "me." There can thus be two kinds of disaster we are talking about, the one that might leave traces as facts (for example finding corpses and ruined buildings etc.) but that could also have been witnessed as a white event, and disasters or events that leave no trace but their own occurrence as an event—such as the event of falling in love, or in hate, an event that leaves no material traces of facts. In the case of the disaster in *Moby-Dick* it, symbolically, has no traces of facts, to emphasize the singularity of the witness to the event.

49. Thus exposing the final dependence of any structure of authority on the sole witness, authorizing his/her own authority.

50. "There is at least one crucial difference between an event of law and an event of art," writes Shoshana Felman. "No matter how dramatic they both are: *a work of art cannot sentence to death*. A trial, unlike art, is grounded in the sanctioned legal violence it has the power (and sometimes the duty) to enact" ("A Ghost in the House of Judgment," p. 152; Felman's emphasis). If authority, at least the one tied to the question of the law, depends either on the power to enact which is, supposedly, given in this case to the court of law by other authorities, or on its own self-institution, which depends on its possi-

bility to authorize itself to use violence, or which uses violence in order to authorize itself, then the helplessness of the work of art can be said to be, from this point of view of its attempt to establish its authority of judgment of truth and fiction, the helplessness of neither being able to enact violence through the authorization given to it by others, since it is usually not given, nor to be itself the institution of violence, since it has no force. The helplessness of the work of literature thus depends on the very fact that other authorities call it a work of literature, that a decision has already been made about whether it is truth or fiction and decided in favor of the second. From this point of view, the depiction of a terrible disaster for which there is a sole witness and which thus cannot rely on any other authority can be seen as, on the one hand, a fantasy of literature to free itself from its own institutionalization, that is, from its own dependence on other authorities which decided its status as fiction, and, on the other hand, its depiction of its own abandoned and helpless state as the one for whom no authority to back up its claims can be found. Thus, Ishmael's attempt to institute himself as authority over truth and fiction can be seen also as an attempt to revolt against the external authorities, which, in advance, seem to have decided the status of his speech.

51. In which case, of course, external authorities that previously decided the status of the work as fictional will have to deny my authority and, in their turn, will have to impose their authority, etc. And thus, we may see, that while it is certainly true, as Felman says in the quote cited above, that there is an essential difference between a trial and a work of art, due to the trial's capacity to sentence to death, this difference is already established from within a certain institutional decision, but against which decision a work of art always poses a threat by, precisely, trying to institute itself as a new origin of authority with its own privileged witnesses which might turn it into a new institution capable of sentencing to death.

52. Obviously, a common rhetorical strategy employed by self-instituting forces is to claim to speak in the name of some other authority, a fictional one (fiction here still understood as a false

claim), thus covering up the violence of their founding act. But perhaps there is something more than the necessary fiction of legitimacy in these claims, for the complex logic of authority proves at its limit not to be able to even claim in whose name it is speaking; there is always the possibility that some other authority is actually speaking from within any self-proclaimed authority.

53. A battle that obviously destroys any clear-cut boundaries that separate the text, the reader, and any other institution, for the battle described at the beginning as raging "within" the text proves to be no less a battle raged "outside" the text, between the reader and other authorities, and also between the reader and the text, other authorities and the text, etc. until it is no longer clear whether it is the "text" speaking from "within" the "reader," or "within" other authorities, or vice versa.

54. "Now small fowls flew screaming over the yet yawning gulf; a sullen white surf beat against its sides; then all collapsed, and the great shroud of the sea rolled on as it rolled five thousand years ago" (p. 572).

55. For Ishmael himself has no authority over his own testimony and cannot be the one validating it for, in a way, he doesn't know at all to what he is witnessing.

56. For I can never know for sure that indeed something happened.

57. At least not truth understood epistemologically as knowledge of truth about facts. It might be that it is a different kind of truth, or perhaps something different from truth altogether.

58. It seems to me, and I say this quite hesitatingly, that this reverberation of the enigmatic scar as a cry into the future is close to, yet somewhat different from, Derrida's understanding of the literary event as that in which singularity and repeatability, or what he calls iterability, are strangely mixed. For Derrida, the transmission of a poem, for example, depends on the one hand on its indecipherable singularity, yet on the other hand on a certain readability of the singular poem, and hence a repeatability of it, which otherwise could not

occur. What I understand as a reverberation of the cry does not assume the possibility of the readability of the poem, but assumes a strange repetition that occurs in the place of the collapse of readability. For Derrida, this structure of literary transmission is similar to the structure of the signature which, on the one hand, is a completely singular mark, yet on the other hand, depends on a recognition and on a legal structure of legitimation and authorization. Yet, as I have tried to show, the wail is that which undermines the legal, conceptual apparatus of legitimation and authorization. Thus if we still want to define the singularity of the whale/wail as a signature, it can never become a signature in the Derridean sense, that is, a signature that can potentially be legally binding.

59. Thus, writing about what I refer to as the traditional concept of authority, Hannah Arendt says: "The authoritarian relation between the one who commands and the one who obeys rests neither on common reason nor on the power of the one who commands; what they have in common is the hierarchy itself, whose rightness and legitimacy both recognize and where both have their *predetermined stable place*." "What Is Authority," in *Between Past and Future: Eight Exercises in Political Thought* (New York: Penguin Books, 1977), p. 93.

60. In relation to this new conception of the authority of the white event, which imposes itself on me and does not involve the authorities governing truth and fiction, we can see one of the major axes along which *Moby-Dick* is a critical reading of Hobbes's *Leviathan*. In his discussion of the issue of miracles, in chapter 37 of the *Leviathan*, Hobbes attempts both to define what a miracle is and to give criteria for distinguishing between false miracles and true ones. "To understand therefore what is a Miracle," writes Hobbes, "we must first understand what works they are, which men wonder at, and call Admirable. And there be but two things which make men *wonder at any event*: The one is, if it be strange, that is to say, such, as the like of it hath never, or very rarely been produced: The other is, if when it is produced, we cannot imagine it to have been done by naturall means, but only by the immediate hand of God." Thomas Hobbes, *Leviathan*

(Cambridge: Cambridge University Press, 1991), p. 300. A further criterion for the miracle, says Hobbes, is "that it be wrought for the procuring of credit to Gods Messengers, Ministers, and Prophets, that thereby men may know, they are *called*, sent, and employed by God, and thereby be the better inclined to obey them" (ibid., p. 301). Finally, arriving at a definition, Hobbes writes: "we may define it thus, A MIRACLE, is a work of God (besides his operation by the way of Nature, ordained in the creation) done, for the *making manifest to his elect*, the mission of an extraordinary Minister for their salvation" (ibid., p. 30). But of course, the definition of the miracle gives rise to the inevitable problem of differentiating a true miracle from a fictive and false one, and distinguishing the miracles, which only God can do, from various strange events that can be produced by the devil, which are, says Hobbes, "but *imposture and delusion*" (p. 304). Hobbes concludes that the only way to decide between a false and true miracle is for the Sovereign authority and judge, God's messenger on earth, to pronounce whether a miracle is true or false: "if a man pretend, that after certain words spoken over a peece of bread, that presently God hath made it not bread, but a God, or a man, or both, and nevertheless it looketh still as like bread as ever it did; there is no reason for any man to think it really done; nor consequently to fear him, till he enquire of God, by his Vicar, or Lieutenant, whether it be done, or not. If he says not, then followeth that which Moses saith . . . he hath spoken it presumptuously, thou shalt not fear him. If he says t'is done, then he is not to contradict it . . . whether the Miracle we hear, or read of, were a reall work, and the Act of a tongue, or pen; but in plain terms, *whether the report be true, or lye. In which question we are not, every one, to make our own private Reason, or Conscience, but the Publique Reason, that is, the reason of Gods supreme Lieutenant, Judge*; and indeed we have made him Judge already, if wee have given him a Sovereign Power, to doe all that is necessary for our peace and defence" (ibid., pp. 305–6). Disregarding, if possible, the religious definition involved in the question of the miracle, it seems to me that the question of the white event is exactly the question of the miracle.

It is an event that is not available to everyone, is strange and wondrous, has to do with being elected, and raises, essentially, the suspicion of delusion and falsity. Hobbes sees no other way but to resort to an authoritarian decision regarding this event, the sovereign is the sovereign over the truth or fictiveness of the miracle, while *Moby-Dick*, we have seen, attempts to bring the whale as precisely the principle of collapse of this Sovereign power, of this Leviathan, by collapsing the epistemic question of its truth or falsity and by trying to make the miracle actually happen, trying to make the white whale/wail heard and witnessed in actuality.

61. The fictional, that is, when it is still understood as not true, for we also want to see the meaning of the fictional change into that which names the trembling together of the testimonial and the fabulous. Also, we might say that it necessarily through the collapse of one understanding of fiction, an epistemic understanding of it in relation to the authoritative categories of truth and falsity, that the new understanding of it as fabulous-testimonial is revealed, a collapse which also reveals its essential resort to the vocabulary of power. That is, I have been trying to describe a process in which there is an event of address, a white wail or cry, which opens up as a relation between the fabulous and the testimonial, yet an event in relation to which a desire for mastery is created which relates to the trembling of the fabulous and the testimonial as having to do with a question of knowledge and tries to treat them as a relation between truth and fiction (understood as false) which it wishes to decide upon. The literary event always tries to make the fabulous-testimonial wail heard by collapsing any attempt of such mastery, yet it is perhaps only from within the experience of a strange undecidability and ambiguity between the truth and the fictional which is discovered in the text, that the address be heard as fabulous-testimony collapsing the previous demand for decision.

62. There is also a third language of power in the novel, which I have not dealt with at all, and it mainly has to do with the various fantasies of omnipotence entertained in relation to the whale/wail.

Bibliography

Agamben, Giorgio. *Homo Sacer: Sovereign Power and Bare Life*. Stanford: Stanford University Press, 1998.
———. *Potentialities—Collected Essays in Philosophy*. Stanford: Stanford University Press, 1999.
———. *Remnants of Auschwitz—The Witness and the Archive*. New York: Zone Books, 1999.
Arendt, Hannah. *Between Past and Future: Eight Exercises in Political Thought*. New York: Penguin Books, 1977.
———. *Totalitarianism*. New York: Harcourt Brace & Co., 1976.
———. *Qu'est-ce que la Politique?* Paris: Editions du Seuil, 1995.
Artaud, Antonin. *Selected Writings*, ed. Susan Sontag. Berkeley and Los Angeles: University of California Press, 1988.
———. *The Theatre and Its Double*, in *Collected Works*, vol. 4, Victor Corti trans. London: John Calder, 1999.
Austin, J. L. *How to Do Things with Words*. Cambridge, Mass.: Harvard University Press, 1978.
Benjamin, Walter. *The Origin of German Tragic Drama*. London and New York: Verso, 1998.
Bezanson, Walter E. "*Moby-Dick*: Work of Art," in *Moby-Dick Cen-*

tennial Essays, ed. Tyrus Hillway and Luther S. Mansfild. Dallas: Southern Methodist University Press, 1953, pp. 30–58.

Blackman, Maurice. "Acting Without Words: Artaud and Beckett and Theatrical Language," *AUMLA: Journal of the Australasian Universities Language and Literature Association* 55 (May 1981): 68–76.

Blanchot, Maurice. *Gaze of Orpheus and Other Literary Essays*. Barrytown: Station Hill Press, 1981.

Bresson, Robert. *Notes on the Cinematographer*. Copenhagen: Green Integer, 1997.

Brodhead, Richard H., ed. *New Essays on Moby-Dick*. Cambridge and New York: Cambridge University Press, 1986.

Brodtkorb, Paul, Jr. *Ishmael's White World: A Phenomenological Reading of Moby Dick*. New Haven: Yale University Press, 1965.

Cadava, Eduardo, Peter Connor, and Jean-Luc Nancy, eds. *Who Comes After the Subject?* New York: Routledge, 1991.

Caruth, Cathy. *Unclaimed Experience: Trauma, Narrative, and History*. Baltimore: Johns Hopkins University Press, 1996.

Cavell, Stanley. "Finding as Founding: Taking Steps in Emerson's 'Experience,'" in *This New Yet Unapproachable America: Lectures After Emerson After Wittgenstein*. Albuquerque: Living Batch Press, 1989.

———. *Disowning Knowledge: In Six Plays of Shakespeare*. Cambridge and New York: Cambridge University Press, 1987.

Celan, Paul. *Collected Prose*. Manchester: Carcanet, 1986.

Chambers, Ross. "'La Magie du réel,' Antonin Artaud and the Experience of the Theatre," *Australian Journal of French Studies* 3 (1966).

Chiaramonte, Nicola. "Antonin Artaud et sa double idée du théâtre," *Preuves: Les Idées Qui Changent le Monde* 205 (1968): 8–17.

Coleridge, Samuel Taylor. *The Complete Poetical Works of Samuel Taylor Coleridge*, ed. Ernest Hartley. Oxford: Clarendon Press, 1975.

Cowan, James C. "Lawrence's Criticism of Melville," *Extracts* (University of Pennsylvania) 17 (1974): 6–9.

De Man, Paul. *Aesthetic Ideology*. Minneapolis: University of Minnesota Press, 1996.

———. *Allegories of Reading: Figural Language in Rousseau, Nietzsche, Rilke, and Proust*. New Haven: Yale University Press, 1979.

Deleuze, Gilles. *Difference and Repetition*. New York: Columbia University Press, 1994.

———. *Essays Critical and Clinical* Minneapolis: University of Minnesota Press, 1997.

———. *Foucault*. Minneapolis: University of Minnesota Press, 1988.

Derrida, Jacques. *Acts of Literature*, ed. Derek Attridge. New York: Routledge, 1992.

———. *Adieu to Emmanuel Levinas*. Stanford: Stanford University Press, 1999.

———. *Demeure: Fiction and Testimony*. Stanford: Stanford University Press, 2000.

———. *Writing and Difference*. London: Routledge, 1997.

Dimock, Wai-Chee. "A Theory of Resonance: Melville and New Historicism," *Melville Society Extracts* (College Station, Tx.) 104 (Mar. 1996).

———. "Ahab's Manifest Destiny," in *Macropolitics of Nineteenth Century Literature: Nationalism, Exoticism, Imperialism*, ed. Jonathan Arac and Harriet Ritvo. Philadelphia: University of Pennsylvania Press, 1991), pp. 184–212.

———. *Empire for Liberty*. Princeton, N.J.: Princeton University Press.

Dryden, Edgar A. "Melville as Poet," *Melville Society Extracts* (Hempstead, N.Y.) 117 (July 1999): 15–18.

Dummett, Michael. "Testimony and Memory," in *The Seas of Language*. Oxford: Oxford University Press, 1997.

Dumoulie, Camille. "Quand les dieux écrivent: Note sur Nietzsche et Artaud," *Roman 20–50: Revue d'Etude du Roman du XXe Siècle* (Lille) 13 (June 1992): 189–97.

———. "L'Acteur selon Artaud ou l'invention du corps," *L'Acteur et son métier*, ed. Didier Souiller and Philippe Baron. Dijon: EUD, 1997.

Felman, Shoshana. *Testimony: Crises of Witnessing in Literature, Psychoanalysis, and History.* New York and London: Routledge, 1992.

———. *The Juridical Unconscious: Trials and Traumas in the Twentieth Century.* Cambridge, Mass.: Harvard University Press, 2002.

———. *Writing and Madness: Literature, Philosophy, Psychoanalysis.* Ithaca: Cornell University Press, 1985.

Fiedelson, Charles, Jr. *Symbolism and American Literature.* Chicago: University of Chicago Press, 1953.

Finter, Helga, and Matthew Griffin. "Antonin Artaud and the Impossible Theatre: The Legacy of the Theatre of Cruelty," *TDR: The Drama Review: A Journal of Performance Studies* 41, no. 4 (156) (Winter 1997): 15–40.

Foucault, Michel. *Discipline and Punish: The Birth of the Prison.* New York: Vintage Books, 1995.

———. *Power*, ed. James Faubion. New York: New Press, 2000.

———. *Power/Knowledge: Selected Interviews and Other Writings, 1972–1977*, ed. Colin Gordon. Brighton, Sussex: Harvester Press, 1980.

———. *The History of Sexuality.* 3 vols. New York: Vintage Books, 1988–90.

Freud, Sigmund. *Group Psychology and the Analysis of the Ego*, ed. James Strachey. New York: W. W. Norton, 1975.

———. *Three Case Histories*, ed., Philip Rieff. New York: Scribner, 1997.

———. *Writings on Art and Literature.* Stanford: Stanford University Press, 1997.

Gasche, Rudolphe. "The Scene of Writing: A Deferred Outset," *Glyph: Johns Hopkins Textual Studies* 1 (1977), pp. 150–71.

Greenblatt, Stephen. *Renaissance Self Fashioning.* Chicago: University of Chicago Press, 1980.

Haar, Michel. *Nietzsche and Metaphysics.* Albany: SUNY Press, 1996.

Hardt, Michael, and Antonio Negri. *Empire.* Cambridge, Mass.: Harvard University Press, 2000.

Hayes, Kevin J., ed. *The Critical Response to Herman Melville's Moby-Dick.* Westport, Conn.: Greenwood Press, 1994.

Heidegger, Martin. *Aristotle's Metaphysics (theta) 1–3: On the Essence and Actuality of Force*. Bloomington: Indiana University Press, 1995.
———. *Being and Time*. Albany: State University of New York Press, 1996.
———. *The Metaphysical Foundations of Logic*. Bloomington and Indianapolis: Indiana University Press, 1992.
Heimonet, Jean-Michel. "Brecht et Artaud: Théâtre et catharsis, I: Psychologie-langage," *Romance Notes* (Chapel Hill, N.C.) 29, no. 3 (spring 1989): 241–50.
Hobbes, Thomas. *Leviathan*. Cambridge: Cambridge University Press, 1991.
Jameson, Frederic. *Brecht and Method*. London and New York: Verso 1998.
Jaworsky, Phillipe *Melville Le Desert et L'Empire*. Paris: Editions rue d'ulm, 1985.
Jehlen, Myra, ed. *Herman Melville—A Collection of Critical Essays*. Englewood Cliffs, N.J.: Prentice Hall, 1994.
Kafka, Franz. *Amerika*, trans. Willa and Edwin Muir. New York: Schocken Books, 1996.
Kazin, Alfred. "Introduction to *Moby-Dick*," in Richard Chase, ed., *Melville: A Collection of Critical Essays*. Englewood Cliffs, N.J.: Prentice Hall, 1962.
Lacan, Jacques. *Ecrits*. Paris: Editions du Seuil, 1970.
———. *Seminar III: The Psychoses*. New York: W. W. Norton, 1993.
Lacoue-Labarthe, Philippe. "Sublime Truth," in Jefferey S. Librett, ed., *Of the Sublime: Presence in Question*. Albany: SUNY Press, 1993.
Lawrence, D. H. *Studies in Classic American Literature*. London: Penguin Books, 1977.
Leclaire, Serge. *Psychoanalyzing*. Stanford: Stanford University Press, 1998.
Levinas, Emmanuel. *Basic Philosophical Writings*, ed. Adriaan T. Peperzak, Simon Critchley, and Robert Bernasconi. Bloomington: Indiana University Press, 1996.

———. *Of God Who Comes to Mind*. Stanford: Stanford University Press, 1998.

———. *Otherwise than Being or Beyond Essence*. Dordrecht/Boston/London: Kluwer Academic Publishers, 1991.

Lingis, Alphonso. *Deathbound Subjectivity*. Bloomington: Indiana University Press, 1989.

Lyotard, Jean-François. *The Differend*. Minneapolis: University of Minnesota Press, 1988.

Maddox, Donald. "Antonin Artaud and a Semiotics of Theater," *Romanic Review* 76, no. 2 (Mar. 1985): 202–15.

Marion, Jean-Luc. *Reduction and Givenness—Investigations of Husserl, Heidegger, and Phenomenology*. Evanston, Ill.: Northwestern University Press, 1998.

Matthiessen, F. O. *American Renaissance: Art and Expression in the Age of Emerson and Whitman*. London and New York: Oxford University Press, 1941.

Melville, Herman. *Confidence Man: His Masquerade*, ed. Hershel Parker. New York: Norton, 1971.

———. *Moby-Dick; Or, The Whale*, ed. Harrison Hayford and Hershel Parker. New York and London: W. W. Norton, 1967.

———. *Moby-Dick; Or, The Whale*, ed. Harrison Hayford, Hershel Parker, and G. Thomas Tanselle. Evanston, Ill.: Northwestern University Press, 2001.

———. *Piazza Tales and Other Prose Pieces*. Chicago: Northwestern University Press, 1987.

———. *The Letters of Herman Melville*, ed. Merrell R. Davis and William H. Gilman. New Haven: Yale University Press, 1960.

Olson, Charles. *Call Me Ishmael: A Study of Melville*. San Francisco: City Light Books, 1947.

Otter, Samuel. *Melville's Anatomies*. Berkeley: University of California Press, 1999.

Pasquier, Pierre. "Athlétisme affectif et ascèse blanche chez Antonin Artaud," *Revue d'Histoire du Théâtre* 34, no. 3 (July–Sept. 1982): 237–48.

Pease, Donald E. "*Moby-Dick* and the Cold War," *The American Ren-*

aissance Reconsidered, ed. Walter Benn Michaels and Donald E. Pease. Baltimore and London: Johns Hopkins University Press, 1985, pp. 113–55.

———. *Visionary Compacts*. Madison: University of Wisconsin Press, 1987.

———. "C. L. R. James, Moby-Dick, and the Emergence of Transnational American Studies," *Arizona Quarterly: A Journal of American Literature, Culture, and Theory* 56, no. 3 (autumn 2000): 93–123.

Pepper, Thomas. *Singularities: Extremes of Theory in the Twentieth Century*. Cambridge and New York: Cambridge University Press, 1997.

Perec, Georges. *W, ou, le souvenir d'enfance*, trans. David Bellos. Boston, Mass.: David R. Godine, 1988.

Plato. *Republic*, trans. Robin Waterfied. Oxford and New York: Oxford University Press, 1993.

Richir, Marc. *Melville—les assises du monde*. Paris: Hachette, 1998.

Sartre, Jean-Paul. "Moby Dick," *Adam International Review* 343–45 (1970): 86–88.

Selby, Nick, ed. *Herman Melville: Moby-Dick—Essays, Articles, Reviews*. New York: Columbia University Press, 1998.

Smock, Ann. "Tongue-Tied: Blanchot, Melville, Des Forets," *MLN* 114, no. 5 (Dec. 1999): 1037–61.

Sollers, Philippe. "La Pensée émet des signes (Artaud)," *Tel Quel* 20 (1965): 12–24.

Spanos, William J. *The Errant Art of Moby-Dick: The Canon, the Cold War, and the Struggle for American Studies*. Durham, N.C., and London: Duke University Press, 1995.

Stanislavsky, Konstantin. *An Actor Prepares*. New York: Theatre Arts Books, 1963.

Tocqueville, Alexis de. *Democracy in America*, ed. J. P. Mayer, trans. George Lawrence. London: Fontana Press, 1994.

Wilson, Eric. "The Nomad, The Pilgrim, and the White Whale," *Colby Quarterly* 34, no. 3 (Sept. 1998): 226–42.

Yim, Chol-Kyu. "Brecht and Artaud as the Theoreticians of the Theatre," *Yonsei Review* (Seoul) 5 (1978): 61–66.

Index

actor, the, 12, 13, 25, 82,125n17. *See also* Brecht; Bresson
address: the question of, 10, 11, 24, 33, 36–58, 67, 68, 73; Ahab as, 80; definition of, as white, 81; as wound, 85; history as, 92
Adorno, Theodor, 2
Agamben, Giorgio, 9, 124n15, 131n9
America, 19–26
Arendt, Hannah, 15, 126n22, 144n24, 147n4, 162n59
Artaud, Antonin, 2–26, 92, 122n9
Austin, J. L., 13
authority: question of, 5–7, 9, 10, 14, 19, 20, 40–49, 83, 122n9, 127n34, 160n52, 161n53; of Ishmael as witness and as storyteller, 104–15, 132n10, 132n11, 158n44; of Melville as writer, 133n14;and the question of literature, 159–60n50, 160n51; traditional concept of, 162n59; Hobbes on, 162–63n60

Benjamin, Walter, 53
Bible, the, 92, 94
Blanchot, Maurice, 1, 8, 141n6
Bloom, Harold, 97, 141n15
body, the, 48–59, 66, 86, 135n2, 136n3, 136–37n5, 139n12, 142n19
Brecht, Bertolt, 125n17
Bresson, Robert, 125n17

canon, question of, 2–3, 127–28n3
Caruth, Cathy, 136–37n5
catastrophe, 4, 8, 9, 19, 121n4
Cavell, Stanley, 22, 126n33, 140n15, 142n21
Celan, Paul, 27, 92, 108
Coleridge, Samuel, Taylor, 38, 92
collapse, 10, 49, 51; of institutional power, 75; of knowledge, 83; of whale investigation, 104; of logic of authority, 120; Ahab's, 139n11
context, question of; political, 18, 19; historical, 24, 25; vs. contextlessness, 90–94, 126n28, 133–34n14

cry, the (also wail, shout, scream) 9, 11, 12, 25, 55–66, 104, 116, 118, 123–24n14, 141n16, 144n25; as white, 77, 84; as wound, 84; Ahab's, 150n7; of literature, 162n58

deconstruction, 2
Deleuze, Gilles, 13, 14, 132n16, 143n22, 148n35, 149n4
De Man, Paul, 13
Derrida, Jacques, 2, 9, 124n15, 131n2, 146n33, 149n4, 153n17, 161n58
Descartes, Rene, 154n4
desire, 59, 60, 80, 117, 124n17, 147n35, 153n17
Dimock, Wai-Chee, 133–34n14
disaster, 3, 4, 8, 11–13, 15, 19–22, 35–37, 41, 45–48, 106, 108, 113, 114, 124n14; as white, 83, 159n4; and the fabulous, 88; and the question of history, 92; witnessing of, 152n15, 160n50
drive, the, 53–55, 60, 62, 69, 80, 97, 98, 115, 117, 139n10, 139n12, 144n24
Dummett, Michael, 124n13

Emerson, Ralph Waldo, 126n33
enigma, 1, 29, 36, 44, 46, 51–53, 57, 58, 134n16; as white, 68, 72, 80, 149n6; Ahab as, 79; of the event, 94
Europe, 19–26
event, the, 9–14, 19, 24, 30, 51, 80, 124n14, 124–25n16, 152n15; as white, 69, 108, 109; as fabulous, 88; actor of the, 125n17; as miracle, 163n60
evil, 53, 150n8, 154n24
excess, 7, 10–13, 20, 21, 24, 39; and whiteness, 80, 83; and the question of history, 93; whale as, 158n41

fabulous, the, 35–46, 58, 82, 83, 86–90, 102, 158n44, 158n45; the opening of language as, 115
Felman, Shoshana, 9, 64, 145n26, 150n7, 159n50, 160n51
fiction, 7, 20, 37, 38, 40, 41, 83, 110, 111, 113; opening of, 154n4; authority over, 160n50, 164n61; new definition of, 164n61
Foucault, Michel, 13, 14, 125n19
freedom, 15, 80, 98, 116–18, 128n35, 151n10, 153n17
Freud, Sigmund, 27, 29, 51, 129n1, 129n2, 134n15, 136n5, 139n12, 144n25, 148n2, 152–53n17

Gasche, Rudolph, 157n32
Greenblatt, Stephen, 16–18

Haar, Michel, 135n18
Hardt, Michael, 128n35
Hawthorne, Nathaniel, 21, 22, 140n15
Heidegger, Martin, 2, 134n17, 144n24, 148n2, 149n4, 153n17
history: the question of, 13, 14, 17, 25, 37, 124n14; literary, 90–98, 141n5; and testimony, 108; as fabulous, 107; distinguished from legend, 110

Index

Hobbes, Thomas, 140n13, 162–64n60
Holderlin, Friedrich, 129n36

Jaworski, Phillipe, 150n9

Kafka, Franz, 25, 129n36
Kazin, Alfred, 31, 33
Kleist, Heinrich Von, 129n36

Lacan, Jacques, 146n34, 153n17
Lacoue-Labarthe, Philippe, 129n2
language, 54–66
Lawrence, D. H., 21, 22, 126n30, 127n34, 128n35
Leclaire, Serge, 139n12, 142n18
Levinas, Emmanuel, 9, 124n15, 126n28, 134n16, 136n4, 142n18, 146n33
life, 2–4, 9, 50, 58, 62, 121n2, 124n12, 135n1, 145n32; of whale, 102, 105, 106, 113
Lingis, Alphonso, 142n18
Lyotard, Jean-François, 9

Marion, Jean-Luc, 134n17
Marx, Groucho, 99
Matthiessen, F. O., 31
meaning, 24, 39–53, 59, 60, 72, 83, 138n6, 139n12, 147n35. *See also* sense
miracle: as political, 15; event as, 163–64n60

Negri, Antonio, 128n35
new-historicism, 2
Nietzsche, Friedrich, 2, 13, 126n29, 135n18

Odyssey, the, 92, 94, 141n16, 145n29
Otter, Samuel, 155n27

passivity, 11, 49, 50, 60, 143n22
pathos, 48, 55, 58, 85, 115, 116, 118
Pease, Donald, 31, 32, 126n31, 132n10, 151n9
Pepper, Thomas, 146n34
Perec, Georges, 155–57n28
performance, performative, 4, 12, 13, 22, 25, 95, 96
Plato, 122n7
Poe, Edgar Allan, 21
power, question of, 2, 3, 13–19, 27–34, 40, 41, 49, 52, 66, 69, 115, 121n3, 126n19, 164n62
political, the, 2, 6, 13–17, 19, 31–33, 61, 125n19

revolution, 11, 15, 24, 40, 46, 80, 124n14; and whiteness, 80, 101, 113
Richir, Marc, 130n8
riddle, 128–30. *See also* enigma

Sartre, Jean-Paul, 2
Schreber, Daniel-Paul, 153n17
sense, question of, 49–52, 56, 138n6. *See also* meaning
Shakespeare, William, 22, 92, 121n1
singularity, 9, 10, 44, 82, 86, 152n15; of the literary work, 95; of Ahab's desire, 147n35. *See also* event, as white
Spanos, William, 151n9
Stanislavsky, Konstantin, 12

testimony, 10, 19, 22, 36, 37, 41, 45, 150n7; to white event, 82, 92
theatre, 4–26, 121n4, 124n12, 125n18
trauma, 38, 136n5

witnessing, 4, 9, 10–13, 20–23, 36, 38, 40, 108, 125n7; Ishmael's, 80, 82; literary history as, 92; the life of whales, 102; of the disaster, 114, 117; of the actor, 159n47
wound, the, 44–59, 84, 85, 136–37n5, 138n6; as white, 77; of history, 95
Wyatt, Thomas, 16–18

The authorized representative in the EU for product safety and compliance is:
Mare Nostrum Group
B.V Doelen 72
4831 GR Breda
The Netherlands

www.ingramcontent.com/pod-product-compliance
Lightning Source LLC
Chambersburg PA
CBHW020801160426
43192CB00006B/401